TIME FOR THE LORD TO ACT

A Catechetical Commentary on the Divine Liturgy

David M. Petras

Foreword by John S. Kachuba

Edited by Fred Saato

Byzantine Catholic
Metropolia of Pittsburgh

Cover: Icon of Christ the High Priest, written by Ilie Hasigan

Quotations from Scripture are taken from the New American Bible, copyright by the Confraternity of Christian Doctrine. Reprinted with permission.

Quotations from the Divine Liturgy of St. John Chrysostom are taken from edition of the Intereparchial Commission for Sacred Liturgy of the Metropolia of Pittsburgh.
Printed in the U.S.A.

Much of the material in this book originally appeared as articles in *The Byzantine Catholic World*.

Distributed by the Byzantine Seminary Press, 3643 Perrysville Avenue, Pittsburgh, PA 15214

ISBN 0-9774069-0-3

Byzantine Catholic
Metropolia of Pittsburgh
66 Riverview Avenue
Pittsburgh, PA 15214-2253

Contents

Foreword

Catechesis for the Divine Liturgy

W hat is Liturgy and why do we place so much importance on it? The word *Liturgy* means "a work of the people" *(Leitourgia)* from two Greek words *laos* and *ergon.* The term *Leitourgia* once indicated a service to and by the people. The Divine Liturgy is not a private act; it is meant to be celebrated within a community. "Christian worship is based on the New Testament revelation of God as a 'community' of Father, Son, and Holy Spirit. When we are baptized into Christ we are made children of the Father and bearers of the Spirit, truly members by extension of the community of the Trinity. Together with all the baptized we are being joined together as a holy temple, 'built together spiritually into a dwelling place for God' (Ephesians 2:22)" (*Light for Life, Part Two, The Mystery Celebrated,* 10, Pittsburgh: God With Us Publications, 1996).

The Divine Liturgy is not a show and not something we just attend passively and witness. We all participate and have a role in the Liturgy: the bishop, the priest, the deacon, the cantor, and all the laity. Since the Liturgy is a living and "breathing" entity, the language in which we pray the Liturgy must also be living and "breathing." Our Church is fortunate that our tradition says that we pray the Liturgy in the vernacular, i.e. the spoken language of the people praying. The Congregation for Oriental Churches on December 10, 1964 approved an official translation of the Liturgy into English. This is the basic translation that has been used until now. Although this translation was basically a good translation, it was found in the last forty years that there were some erroneous passages and in some areas the style could be improved. The bishops of our Church felt that instead of just making cosmetic changes, a thorough review of the text and rubrics would be in order. An Inter-eparchial Liturgy Commission was established to complete this work. After a review by our bishops the revised text was sent to the Sacred Congregation for Oriental Churches in Rome. The Sacred Congregation approved this text, along with the changes suggested by scholars in Rome, on March 31, 2001.

It is hoped that with the revised translation and changes in the rubrics, the Divine Liturgy that we all pray, and that is so essential to our lives, will take on a more significant role for us. The following catechesis is meant to bring us clearer understanding and an appreciation of the Divine Liturgy. Along with this understanding and uniformity in the celebration of the Liturgy, we can grow spiritually and concentrate on the Liturgy and not compare the differences between how the Liturgy is celebrated in one place or another. By hearing the gospel and epistle readings, by listening to the prayers of the priest read aloud, by participating in the Eucharist, by praying together in the Divine Liturgy, we share the Mysteries of our Lord with all believers and members of the Body of Christ, the Church. When we leave the Church building and take into our lives what we have learned and experienced in the Divine Liturgy, then we truly live a communal life in Christ. The Liturgy cannot remain a once-a-week event; it will be part and partial to our lives every day. When we implement the Divine Liturgy in our lives then Liturgy truly becomes a work of the people of God.

Mitred Archpriest John S. Kachuba

Introduction

Liturgical Reform in the Byzantine Church

The Second Vatican Council has reminded us that the Church is always in need of reform. Reform often feels like one of the most difficult processes to go through, and, yet, here the Church is saying that it is a permanent part of its existence. The difficulty with reform, for many, is that it seems to put people through constant upset and change. It makes it seem that there is no fixed point, no secure foundation, in an ever-changing world. It seems to be opposed to Jesus Christ, whom, Scripture tells us, "is the same yesterday, today and forever" (Hebrews 13:8). Many, therefore, but still a minority in the Church, resist accepting the Second Vatican Council and its call to reform.

The Council Fathers were exactly right, that reform is a constant part of the life of the Church. While our Lord, Jesus Christ, Son of God, is completely free of sin and has no need of reform, we remain sinners still in need of purification and sanctification. In our individual spiritual lives, we must examine ourselves every day, to see whether we are following faithfully on the path of the Gospel, or whether we have fallen into the wrong path, and have become guilty of faults and misdeeds. Similarly, the whole Church, being as it is, made up of many individual human beings, none of whom are perfect, must continually examine itself to see if it is following in the paths of the Gospel. This is the first part of reform.

If we have failed to follow the path of the Gospel, the next step is to find ourselves back to the true way. Sometimes we conceive of reform as innovation: something new that is being thrust upon the Church. True reform, though, is a return: reshaping our behavior, our actions, our institutions and structures so that they conform to the will of God in the Gospel. This need is always present, not because our Lord or His Gospel changes, but because our needs and the structures of the world in which we live are constantly changing. Structures that once were life-giving in a different kind of society can become oppressive. To remain faithful to the Gospel might mean we have to change the way the message of Christ is applied, and this may be difficult or painful.

The most important form of Christian activity is the Liturgy, in which we offer a sacrifice of praise to God and are brought into the life of the Trinity. Roman Catholics often praise the Byzantine Liturgy for its "venerable antiquity." It is true that the Eastern Churches are more conservative and maintain better certain Christian principles going back to the early centuries of the faith, but at the same time the reality of change in response to the needs of the people must also be acknowledged. The Liturgy is a living tradition, always adapting to the needs of the world in which we live, while remaining faithful to the precepts of our Lord to "do this in memory of me."

Liturgical Change through the Ages

Adapting the Liturgy is not something new. Throughout the centuries, various aspects of the Liturgy have developed and changed, though many are reluctant to admit this. Our own personal experience of liturgical change is very limited. It has been over two thousand years since Christ, and, on the average most of us have lived for only two to three percent of that time. Since it is not a direct part of our experience, it is very difficult for us to know how our great-grandparents and more distant ancestors actually worshiped. Therefore, for many, "ancient Liturgy" is "how it was done when we were children" or what our parents told us. However, this is simply not true.

In fact, since the Emperor Constantine did not establish his capitol in the ancient town of Byzantium until the beginning of the fourth century, we cannot even speak of a "Byzantine Liturgy" before that time. Then, it followed the general format of any

Christian Eucharist — the entrance into the church, the reading of scripture and homilies on it, the prayer of intercession for the people, the bringing in of the gifts of bread and wine, the prayer of offering or consecration over these gifts, and their distribution in Holy Communion, for they had become the body and blood of our Lord. Every Christian Liturgy does the same basic thing, though each with its own style.

When the new city of Constantinople, formerly Byzantium, began to develop its own Liturgy in the fourth century, it, of course, had to follow the basic form commanded by Jesus and also borrowed elements from neighboring Churches. The anaphora (prayer of offering) of St. John Chrysostom was adopted from the Church at Antioch and that of St. Basil from Cappadocia.

Liturgical reform was sought by Justinian in the sixth century, by Theodore of Andidum in the eleventh century, by the Kollyvades monks in the eighteenth century, because the Church, and the center of its life, the Liturgy, is always in need of reform. St Theodore the Studite, in the ninth century, had to reform the monasteries of Constantinople after iconoclasm. He adopted the liturgy of the Monastery of St. Sabbas in the Holy Land, believing this to be the most accurate reflection of the Gospel, which came from Jerusalem.

Until the fifteenth century, the only way to transmit the text of the Liturgy was through hand-written manuscripts. Because of this, there were many more variations in the Liturgy, since anyone could commission a manuscript as they wished. Therefore, many different eparchies and monasteries, while certainly following the same basic form, had many variations in the rites they used. At the same time, all churches that were under the jurisdiction of the Patriarch of Constantinople used the ritual of that city, with minor differences.

As time passed, the churches in Slav-speaking territories and in Greek-speaking territories followed somewhat different versions of the basic Byzantine Liturgy. This changed with the invention of the printing press. Now it was possible to mass-produce liturgical books, which would all be exactly the same. From this time, in both West (after the Council of Trent) and the East (after the fall of Constantinople) the Liturgy became more rigid, because printed books, all the same, were easily and cheaply available. With the invention of the printing press, liturgical books were now able to achieve a uniformity that would last for centuries. Indeed, the idea that we cannot change the text of the Liturgy as it has been handed down to us still persists, even though the detailed tradition only comes from the invention of printing.

The Slavonic Liturgy

In the middle of the seventeenth century, the Russian Patriarch Nikon embarked on a reform of the Liturgy. This was truly meant as a "reform," because he intended consciously to return the Liturgy to its more ancient basis by imitating exactly the liturgical books of the Greek Church, which he considered as apostolic and therefore more in touch with the original gospel of Christ than the Slavs, converted to Christianity only in the tenth century. Nikon's goal was to make the Russian Liturgy conform exactly to the Greek Liturgy, which he saw as the modern continuation of the apostolic forms of worship. Nikon's purpose was noble; however, he was wrong in thinking that the Greek Church had never changed or that it in fact preserved a more ancient tradition than the Slavs.

Because of the printing press, what Nikon accomplished was to become the model for the Russian Liturgy until the present time. Nikon's reform had a great effect on all the Byzantine Churches, including the Ukrainian and Ruthenian Church, which only recently had entered into communion with Rome, because Russia was still the largest of the Slav nations and had the most resources, including printing presses. At least until the art of printing spread throughout Europe, all the Slav Churches still got their books from Russia.

Nikon's reform also probably caused a preservative reaction among the Russian clergy and people, since the reform itself provoked a division within the Russian Church. A sizable minority of the people and clergy (though no bishops) refused to accept Nikon's work, and separated themselves from the Patriarchal Church, taking the name "Old Believers." The Russian Church has been very suspicious of any liturgical modification since that time; one factor may be a fear of provoking another schism.

At first, Byzantine Catholics had continued to use the Orthodox liturgical books, changing only the names of the patriarchs and bishops they commemorated. Therefore, most of the new Greek Catholic Churches also accepted the reform of Nikon, though, interestingly, they sometimes maintained some of the minor practices of the "Old Believer" Church. After the time of Nikon the Liturgy in the Greek Catholic Churches changed, in some ways very dramatically, after they were able to possess their own printing presses. Sadly, the force that was driving these changes was a common presumption that Western European culture was far superior to the Byzantine tradition, because the West had an overwhelming spirit of progress, the best schools and universities, and the power of science and technology. This perception of Western superiority led the Byzantine Catholics in union with Rome to modify the Liturgy to appear outwardly more like the Latin Mass. This process was called "latinization" and it resulted in the removal of icon screens, Communion distributed kneeling, small hand bells, organs, altars placed against the wall, liturgies that were read and not sung, altar missals, the denial of Communion to young children, the service of Benediction, the rosary and Stations of the Cross and many others. In some places and times, even the use of unleavened bread and Roman style vestments were introduced, but these did not become as widespread. All this happened out of a feeling of inferiority, that the Eastern tradition was less valuable than the Western. This distorted rather than reformed the Liturgy, because it was done for cultural reasons that were outside an authentic liturgical spirituality and theology.

In 1720, the Synod of Zamosc was held, which attempted to put a check on most of these "latinizations," but it ultimately failed. The Archbishop of Polotsk, Heraclius Lisovsky, also attempted a reform at the end of the eighteenth century, but this, too, failed, for personal and political reasons. It has been the bane of Eastern Catholic history that cultural and political forces have shaped the liturgy more than spiritual and theological principles. When Russia and Austro-Hungary partitioned Poland at the end of the eighteenth century, any Greek Catholic eparchies that fell into Russian territory were forced or induced back into the Orthodox communion. As a reaction, in those eparchies that remained in Catholic Austria-Hungary, there was another wave of latinization, this time as a defense against Russian assimilation. To make a distinct Catholic-Orthodox hybrid rite was seen as a way to justify the existence of a Byzantine Catholic Church. Again political forces dictated liturgical practice. Among the Eastern Catholics who immigrated to the United States, cultural forces, and the impetus to conform to what seemed to be more "American," but was actually Western European, continued to deform the Liturgy for the wrong reasons.

The Second Vatican Council called upon the Eastern Catholic Churches to reform themselves and to restore their genuine heritage. This does not mean going back to what the Patriarch Nikon did in the seventeenth century, but it does mean — and with some pain to all of us — rediscovering our authentic Tradition that will lead us to Christ. To say simply that whatever we are doing is "our tradition" and that nothing need be changed is to ignore the fact that not everything done in the past is a part of the authentic Tradition. Our Church, now as always, must examine its conscience to see if it has been faithful to the Gospel as it has been developed and expressed in the Tradition. This requires discernment and wisdom, which are gifts of the Holy Spirit and not expressions of our own personal wishes and desires. It is certain that one way in which the Holy Spirit acts is in the guidance of the Church.

The Council's call does empower our Church to again respond to the pastoral needs of its people to recover a Liturgy that more clearly leads us to God through Christ in the power of the Holy Spirit. Since the Council, much of this work has been done, but much still remains.

Should the Liturgy be Shorter?

When I was a young priest studying the Liturgy, I once made a trip to Slovakia to visit my grandparents' villages. We had to pass through Prague. I was there on a Sunday, and my friend and I found a Greek Catholic Church and attended the Divine Liturgy there. The pastor appreciated our visit and took us out for breakfast. He asked me what I was studying in Rome. When I told him, "Liturgy," he leaned closer to me and asked, "Can you please tell me how to make the Liturgy shorter?"

Over the past three decades, I have found this to be one of the prime concerns of priests and people in our Church. The desire to make the Liturgy as short as possible comes from the not completely conscious idea that attending the Liturgy is only an obligation we have to do to be in the divine good will. The Liturgy has little value in itself and the time spent in the Liturgy is boring. The quicker it is performed, the better. Today, though, this strictly legalistic attitude is less common.

Our perception of the Liturgy has been affected by the way we learn truth, or, to put it in more secular terms, the way reality is presented to us. In our Church, the icon is the window into reality, but in the society in which we live, television has become our window into the world. This touches the lives of every person, even those few who react against it and refuse to watch it. There is, of course, nothing intrinsically evil about television, for it is a gift of God, but like every benefit given us we are able to distort its value. I don't mean simply the content of what is shown on television, but the very medium itself. By its very nature, it can make it more difficult for us to distinguish between reality and fiction. A television story can take on the feel of reality, while reality can become like just another story. More than that, it makes entertainment the most significant life value, and the Liturgy, which is not entertainment but communion with God, becomes judged by those same standards. Since television shows last about an hour, an hour becomes the maximum time a Liturgy can take, and if the quality of our worship is not "entertaining" enough, it will seem much longer.

The bigger question is, what is the place of the Liturgy in our life of faith? Our great-grandparents devoted more time to Liturgy, often two hours or more, and it was the most important thing they did during the week. We tend to view them as primitive and backward; however, they may have had more wisdom than we do. One of the Fathers of the Church once said that we need two hours of prayer to come into the presence of God. Again, I am very much aware that this will not be acceptable to modern sensitivities attuned to television's one-hour time frame, but we should be humble enough to admit that our faith in God and desire for God is weaker. At the same time, I am encouraged that there has been some restoration since the time of my youth. Then, a generation or two ago, everyone was into minimalism, and the shorter Liturgy was the ideal. Since then, we have recovered an appreciation for spirituality somewhat, though we often separate it from liturgical worship and connect it with our individual relationship to God.

Any Church that would hold that the shorter its Liturgy is, the better, is obviously dead. If we claim this, we are saying that our greatest value, being in the presence of our Lord, is valueless, and there is nothing more. The Liturgy is not entertainment, though that is the way many see it, and the mega-churches that provide shows for its congregations are growing. Liturgy is community, and that means it requires our active participation, joining with people that sometimes make us feel uncomfortable and enduring moments in which we are bored, that is to say, not entertained. As community, Liturgy often demands work and commitment, difficult values for a culture dominated by modern entertainment media.

Certainly, at the same time, the Liturgy does not have to be as boring as possible. The faithful have the right to hear the Gospel clearly, and to be blessed with at least sincere Christian preaching, even if all priests do not have the same rhetorical abilities. The various activities of the Liturgy — words of prayer, ritual, gestures, symbols, music, art — should be done as well as possible. If they fall below minimal standards, then we have to work and practice to make them better. The Liturgy is the work of God, but if we do not pour our faith into it, it will become an empty gesture and will not sanctify us.

The pouring of hot water into the chalice before Communion may be a symbol of this, for it represents the warmth of our faith. Pouring the water, the priest says, "The fervor of faith, full of the Holy Spirit." The Liturgy for us is always the presence of Christ, transforming by the Spirit the gifts of bread and wine that we offer into His body and blood. The hot water does not change the gifts, but it indicates that we must be willing to put our whole faith into the worship that we offer to the Lord. If we bring faith to the Liturgy, then time becomes of less importance, and eventually disappears altogether.

Can the Liturgy Be Made More Practical?

The dictionary definition of "practical," is that which is "concerned with the application of knowledge to useful ends." The dictionary then goes on to explain that practical "stresses effectiveness as tested by actual experience or as measured by a completely realistic approach to life or the particular circumstances involved." The question I would like to ask is what do we mean when we speak about the Liturgy being "practical." In a certain sense, it would seem to be "impractical" from the beginning. In no way does it deal with "everyday affairs," but instead carries us into eternal and infinite realities. It requires us to budget time and effort to receive, on one level, what seems to be a little bit of bread and wine, but has become the body and blood of Christ.

An action can be practical on two different levels. On the first level, something is practical when it is simple, easy and realistic. This is what we usually mean by practical. The problem is that it is also possible to simplify the Liturgy to the point where its ultimate goals are distorted or omitted. On the second level, though, something "practical" is the application of knowledge to a useful end. The "knowledge" here is the nature of the Liturgy: a divine mystery that makes God's saving grace present in order to bring us human beings into God's life. Whatever facilitates this goal, then, is useful or practical.

This is understandable even in ordinary daily existence. For example, there might be a grocery store a mile from our house. Suppose that we need a loaf of bread and a quart of milk. On one level, the quickest and most practical solution might be to get into our car and drive to the store, which would take a few minutes at most. On another level, if we have a plan of daily exercise for the sake of our health that includes a daily two-mile walk, it might be more practical to combine our exercise with the errand and walk to the store to pick up our needed items. The same is true in the Liturgy: in order to decide what is truly "practical" it might be best to keep in mind its ultimate goals.

Some examples might be helpful for understanding. Baptism is the sacramental mystery of our entrance into the life of the Holy Trinity and simultaneously, because Christ is one of the Trinity, into the Church, which is the Body of Christ. As such, we are baptized into the pattern of Jesus' life. St. Paul heard His challenge — "Whoever wishes to come after me must deny himself, take up his cross and follow me" (Mark 8:34) — and explained it further, "We were indeed buried with him through baptism into death, so that, just as Christ was raised from the dead by the glory of the Father, we too might live in newness of life" (Romans 6:4). On one level, the "most practical" way to baptize would be to pour a few drops of waters on the candidate's head, but on the second level, immersion in water would be more practical to manifest the meaning of baptism as dying and rising in Christ.

Another example might be the reading of Scriptures in Church. The ultimate practicality — which as far as I know, has not been seriously proposed — would be to have all the faithful read the text privately in their pew. Again, though, this is not "practical" because the goal of the Scripture reading is that the Good News be proclaimed to the assembly. Few liturgical moments can be more powerful than a clear and meaningful declamation of the word of God. The Scripture should be read even if most of the congergation is literate, and this public reading should be done by those of the congregation most capable of doing so.

At the same time, those who have other roles and tasks in the Liturgy sometimes ignore the reading in order to get their tasks done in a timely, "practical" manner. However, this is not "practical" if it detracts from the central importance of the word of God in the community and in our lives. The Church has always considered the Gospel one of the most important parts of our liturgical worship. It has therefore bound these sacred words in precious covers and on quality paper. Though it might seem "practical" to read the words from a pamphlet or bulletin, this false "practicality" cheapens the value of the message.

To conclude, "practicality" takes its meaning from the goals we set for ourselves. If our goals are minimal, then "practicality" means doing what is simplest and quickest. On the other hand, if we seek to make the symbols and message of the Liturgy mean what they are supposed to express, then it will become "practical" to enact the rituals with greater grace and fidelity to tradition. We might object that all this is the concern of the clergy, especially of the priest and pastor. However, it is also the concern of all the people, some of whom may discourage the clergy from a more meaningful celebration for their own reasons, such as a desire for shortness in services, lack of interest or even an embarrassment in ceremony.

Why Change Our Translation of the Liturgy?

The Byzantine Liturgy has been expressed in many languages. Throughout the centuries, one of its strengths has been the principle that worship should be in the language of the people (even though Church Slavonic and Koine Greek have long ceased to be the spoken forms of these languages). Thus the Byzantine Church allowed the use of Slavonic in the Liturgy in the Slav missions, and it also permitted Georgian in the Church of Georgia, which remained in union with Constantinople, and also Arabic for those Churches in the Middle East that remained faithful to Constantinople, after the Moslem conquest.

Theodore Balsamon, who lived in the twelfth century, the most famous of all the Eastern canonists, formulated the Byzantine principle regarding liturgical languages: "Those who are wholly Orthodox, but who are altogether ignorant of the Greek tongue, shall celebrate in their own language, provided only that they have exact versions of the customary prayers, translated on to rolls and well written in Greek characters." The provision about Greek characters is, of course, unreasonable, but the Byzantine Church has continued to pride itself on the principle of the vernacular, despite the fact, that no translations into modern Russian or Greek have yet been permitted.

In the latter half of the seventeenth century, translation of the Liturgy into Romanian was permitted and in the nineteenth century Byzantine Catholics translated the Liturgy into Hungarian. In 1896, even after the Liturgy was in fact being celebrated in Hungarian, Rome forbade the translation, holding again that "ancient languages are better for maintaining the dignity of sacred rites" because "living languages change every day." There was much opposition to the Roman prohibition, and the celebration of the Liturgy in Hungarian continued.

In the United States our bishops and priests were aware of the Byzantine principle on the vernacular. The Liturgy began to be celebrated in English, probably in the Youngstown area in the late 1940's. It spread quickly in the early 1950's. In 1955, the popular Bishop Fulton Sheen celebrated the Liturgy in English at Uniontown, drawing attention to the idea that vernacular was the future for the Liturgy in America. At first, some Roman Catholic bishops objected but opposition to the vernacular collapsed after the Second Vatican Council. In 1964, the Sacred Oriental Congregation approved an English translation of the Divine Liturgy for our Church.

Translation from one language to another always presents problems. One of the greatest translators of the Bible, St. Jerome, wrote, "If I translate word by word, it sounds absurd; if I am forced to change something in the word order or style, I seem to have stopped being a translator." It is not possible to translate exactly from one language to another because words do not perfectly overlap in meaning. Likewise languages do not exist in isolation from a particular culture and human context. Words simply are not going to mean the same thing for a society in the atomic age as they did for the ancient Romans. Any translation will involve some interpretation of the original. The point of translation is to reproduce in the received language the same meaning and the same effect as the original. This requires art and intelligence, and for this reason, we will probably always argue about translations.

I think two principles are of primary importance. The first is that a liturgical text must be uplifting. Pope Paul VI said in 1965 that the liturgical text "should always be worthy of the noble realties it signifies, set apart from the everyday speech of the street and the marketplace." Understanding of the text, however, must be the primary consideration, believing that they do convey a real meaning that is most relevant to our lives and will transform them. And so Pope Paul VI said that the vernacular liturgical texts should be "within the grasp of all, even children and the uneducated."

Why Are More Prayers Being Said Aloud?

When a man is ordained a priest, the bishop clothes him in the vestments of his new office. Each time one of the vestments is given, the people sing, "Axios," the Greek word for "He is worthy." The very last article that the bishop gives in Slav-Byzantine Churches is a book called the liturgikon, which contains the texts of the prayers that the priest says during the celebration of the Divine Liturgy.

In the beginning of the life of the Church, the apostles and their successors tried to follow Christ's command and pray as He did at the Last Supper. At this early stage, they followed no written texts but improvised their prayers, as long as they followed the traditional pattern conforming to the thanksgiving offered by Jesus at the Last Supper.

As the Church began to grow not every bishop or priest had the same talents in composing prayers. Some used the prayers to express their own ideas, not in conformity with the teaching and traditions of the Church. At the same time, more expressive texts composed by holy men and theologians came into greater use. It is now believed that some of the very ancient anaphoras ("prayers of offering") that we have were models that the bishop or presbyter could use to construct his own prayer.   Among these is the Anaphora of the Twelve Apostles that was used by St. John Chrysostom when he became Archbishop of Constantinople. It is his elaboration of this prayer that has come down to us as the Anaphora (Liturgy) of St. John Chrysostom.   In time the Church allowed less and less freedom in what prayers were to be said. Eventually the priest was required to use only prayers already approved by the Church.   The priest was expected to pray from the book and not make up his own texts.

Even when the Prayer of Offering was said in a spontaneous manner by the presiding priest or bishop, the people would confirm it by their "Amen." As the prayers became fixed additional popular interjections were added so that John Chrysostom could speak of the priest and people as "speaking for one another" in their alternating of this prayer.

The prayers of the Liturgy were said aloud until the fifth century. Why did the prayers become silent? We don't know, but perhaps part of the problem was the change in the vernacular language.   In English, for example, we now have difficulty understanding Shakespeare's plays, written many centuries ago. As the spoken language changed and that of the prayers stayed the same, they became incomprehensible to the average person.

Another reason might be that over time the order of deacon has been eclipsed and the priest has taken over the major tasks of the deacon: saying the litanies, incensing the church and reading the Gospel. The litanies, which called for the continuous responses of the people, had to chanted aloud. Since the people only answered "Amen" at the end of the priestly prayers, most of these prayers could be read quietly with only the last phrases aloud. Priests, in effect, had abandoned their own role in the liturgy to take up the deacon's role. Therefore, in the course of history, the most impor-tant element of the priests' role has become silent:

The translation of the Liturgy into the vernacular and the restoration of the order of deacon has forced that situation to change. Priests will again have to learn to be good proclaimers. The people's hymns are a worthy part of the Liturgy, for our spiritual worship is the giving of glory to God. The deacon's petitions are also a worthy part of the Liturgy, for our total dependence on God for "every good and perfect gift" (James 1:17) is also a part of our true religion. It is the prayers said by the priest in the people's name, however, that bring us into the very center of the mystery.

Here we stand before God, the Creator, "who has brought us from non-existence into being." Here we are swept up into a host of thousands of archangels and tens of thousands of angels, cherubim and seraphim. We hear again that God loves the world with such intensity that He sent His only Son, "so that everyone who believes in Him should not perish but have life everlasting." As we hear this prayer, echoing through the centuries, we sit with Christ at the mystical table, we recognize Him in the bread and cup as did the disciples at Emmaus. And our prayer responds to the mystery as did Job's: "I know that you can do all things and that no purpose of yours can be hindered ... I had heard of you by word of mouth, but now my eye has seen you" (Job 42:1.3).

One might object that the prayers are too difficult for the people to understand and just add time to the Liturgy. I simply do not accept this. Most of the congregation is certainly intelligent enough to understand them, and their language is no more difficult than many of the Scripture readings or hymns, or perhaps even the homilies. Writing in around the year AD 600, John Moschos told the story of a group of boys that had memorized the anaphora from hearing it said aloud. Obviously, these prayers impress many people and I agree entirely with Father Taft that their public recitation adds to and does not detract from the mystery, "Long after all the prayers have been heard and studied, and all the theologians have had their say, the divine mysteries remain mysteries because of their very nature, and not because we seek to make them unintelligible by hiding them under a camouflage of silence!" In all the Churches of the East, Orthodox and Catholic, that use the vernacular, the priestly prayers are being restored for public hearing.   I believe there can be no reform, nor even a whisper of a reform of the Liturgy, without this restoration.

Will the Priest Now Face the People?

In the Byzantine Church, the tradition has been that everyone present prays facing the East, the direction of light, for the sun comes from the East.   Now it is true that not all our churches actually face the Eastern direction, so what this means is that the priest and the congregation all pray facing the Holy Table, the altar.

St. John of Damascus gives us a theological reason for facing the East: "When [Jesus] was received again into heaven He was carried towards the East and His apostles worshiped Him, and therefore He will come again in the way they beheld Him going towards heaven; as the Lord Himself said. 'As the lightning comes out of the East and shines to the West, so also shall the coming of the Son of Man be.'   So, in expectation of His coming we worship towards the East."

Today in the Roman Church the people pray facing the altar, while the priest prays facing the people.   No rule on the direction of prayer was given in the Vatican II Decree on the Liturgy itself.   The instruction on implementing the decree, *Inter Oecumenici*, that came out in September, 1964, nine months after the first session, simply states, "It is licit to celebrate the Mass facing the people" (¶ 95).   More in the United States than in Europe, this practice has become a defining standard.   Any church that does not follow it is labeled as old-fashioned and extremely conservative.   Once when I met a pair of Roman priests and explained who I was, they responded, "Oh yes, we know, you're the Church where the priest keeps his back to the people."   This new practice has also had a great influence on our Catholic brethren of the Maronite and some other Oriental communities, who probably follow this new practice more often than not.

I think that the practice of the priest facing the people is a liturgical mistake, and that our Church would do well to retain its tradition.   One of the theological reasons for permitting this, not stated explicitly here, was to emphasize that the Liturgy was indeed a meal, and that the family of the Church was gathered around the Holy Table to partake of the sacred food of the holy body and blood of our Lord. The reason most offered today for the practice is that the priest should not turn his back to the people. To do so seems to be a breach of hospitality. This has become so ingrained now that to do otherwise would seem to be a great insult. However, this carries with it a certain presumption that could be misinterpreted, and this is that the priest is the host of the Liturgy. Of course, at any banquet, if the host were to turn his back on the people he invited, it would be a breach of manners. The problem is that in our liturgical service, the priest is not the host. This may be seen in Holy Communion. In a secular banquet, the host will serve food to his guests first and then partake himself at the end. However, in the Liturgy, the priest takes Communion first. This is because he is not the host. The true host at every Liturgy is our Lord Jesus Christ, who gives himself in Communion to all the people, beginning with the one who presides, the bishop or priest.

It was much easier in the Roman tradition to elevate the role of the priest. In Western theology, the priest is often called, in Latin, *alter Christus*, "another Christ." When he administrates the sacramental mysteries, he pronounces formulas in his own name. Therefore, in the Roman rite, the priest says, "I baptize you," while in the Byzantine tradition, the priest prays in the passive voice, "The servant of God is baptized." It is not that the faith is different, but that the role of the human being who shares in the priesthood of our Lord and God and Savior Jesus Christ is accented more in the West than in the East. However, in both the same reality is present, and the power and grace and redemption come through Jesus Christ, through the Holy Spirit, for in God alone resides all power, glory and honor. St. John Chrysostom, in speaking of the words of Christ used in the Divine Liturgy, stated that the human priest "stands in the place of Christ." The words are pronounced by a human being, but the power is God's. Because of the difference in emphasis in the two theological traditions, it is more difficult in the Eastern Church for the priest to take the position of host.

Though certainly it is not intended, the position of the priest facing the people can be misinterpreted to diminish the central role of the presence of God in the worshiping community. Once, in fact, a priest explained to me that Jesus died on the cross, and that now he lived in him, the priest! It seems ironic to me that now some Roman Catholics, criticize Eastern priests for "having their backs to the people," when in actuality, the Byzantine priest is being more democratic: priest and people together praying facing the presence of our Lord on the altar.

For Your Reflection

1. Many Western Christians see liturgical renewal as making worship more contemporary. How are the Eastern Churches renewing their liturgical life?

2. List the examples of latinization or delatinization you have experienced in any of our churches. What do you think prompted the adoption of these measures?

3. What makes a liturgical usage "practical" according to this chapter?

One — Liturgy and Spirituality

People often say that they go to church and attend the Liturgy in order to find a spiritual life. Spirituality is a kind of buzzword today, and even in a casual trip to the store we can find many books on the subject. It is a mysterious word expressing something that we thirst for as human beings. Spirituality is also an abstract word open to much interpretation. It is used in many different ways. One thing is certain: it has very little to do with ceiling repairs, leaky faucets, trash collection, and other daily problems.

In the last few centuries, human knowledge has developed a preference for concrete, physical knowledge in the sciences and the spiritual side of human life has been eclipsed. We have focused on the "hands on" world that we can touch, feel, smell, taste and see. Technology seeks to understand this world, to measure the distance to the stars, to find the edge of the universe: in short "to grasp all creation in our hand, to understand exactly what it is and how it works" in the words of the prominent physicist Stephen Hawking. We want to make the world work for us, and perhaps in this way even to achieve an otherwise elusive immortality.

It is this pursuit and this concentration on unlocking the secrets of the "hands on" universe that has made the spiritual universe — which is seen only with the eyes of the soul, and which we enter every time that we step into church and raise a song of praise to God with our bodily lips — seem to be somehow less real: perhaps even a myth, a fairy tale or a mental construct. All of us — priests and faithful — must humbly admit this and come to grips with it. Each and every one of us is affected by the technological vision of the world. Because we have torn the atom apart and attempted to enter the mind of the Creator, the vision of our people and our own visions have changed.

Sometimes people tend to imagine the spiritual world as a kind of parallel universe with its own land, buildings, and places that exist side-by-side with the world we actually live in, touch, see and hear. The spiritual world is concerned with what we do in church; the "real world" is where we live the rest of our lives and the two really don't touch one another.

There are not parallel worlds. St. Maximos the Confessor was very realistic about this. The Church is the soul of the world and spirituality means seeing the real world in a new perspective. It means seeing our total reality with new eyes, as God sees it. If we say there are five bodily senses (though there are really more), and there is an intuitive "sixth sense" of mind and will, then the seventh and perfect sense is to see with the eyes of God.

To understand our worship of God, and why we pray and sing the way we do, we must understand Christian spirituality. An authentically Christian spirituality is not the product of imagination. Since God cannot be imagined, any concepts of God we devise are inadequate. The only true image of God is Jesus the Messiah. "God spoke to us through a son, ...who is the refulgence of his glory, the very imprint of his being, and who sustains all things by his mighty word" (Hebrews 1:1-3). Jesus entered our "real world," lived in it and transformed it. This is why we depict the spiritual world in icons that we can see and touch.

The Liturgy is our rite of entrance into this world, as witnessed by the Church. "What was from the beginning, what we have heard, what we have seen with our eyes, what we have looked upon and touched with our hands concerns the Word of life." (1 John 1:1). It is our experience of the life in Christ that we entered by baptism and chrismation. Technology is one kind of knowledge and we have used it to recreate the world in which we live so that we are always warm and fed and clothed. We have visibly transformed the planet and made it into our own human habitat through our sense of perception. Liturgy is the entry into yet another world, a world a truly divine and human habitat. We not only cloth and feed our bodies but also our souls, not by way of fairy tales or figments of imagination nor by way of a false division where we leave the secular world to the technocrats and take what is left, but by way of a co-operation with God in creating His blessed Kingdom.

When we see with the eyes of faith, it is like seeing with the eyes of God. We, as human beings, see in the color of icons, an image of the splendor of God. When we hear the word of praise, a joyful sound to the Lord, and when we smell the fragrance of incense, an offering to the Lord, and when we taste and see how good the Lord is in Holy Communion, this is spirituality. We discover a new world, the world of the Spirit.

Liturgy and Mystery

A common saying is "everybody loves a mystery," because mysteries challenge us, amuse us, and even scare us. Yet, we must all confess to occasionally turning to the end of a mystery novel to see how it all turns out. A mystery that remains unsolved is not very satisfying.

There is a dimension of mystery to our faith that is also fascinating and fearful. Many people want to attend church where there is a sense of mystery, and are drawn to our Church, which has this quality of mystery. We speak of the Eucharist as a mystery. Before Communion we pray: "Accept me as a partaker of your mystical supper, O Son of God; for I will not reveal your mystery to your enemies." How is the Eucharist a mystery? Is it the inscrutable ceremonies or incomprehensible language, which many seek, that make the Liturgy mysterious? Or is it something deeper which is hidden in this mystery and which gives meaning to our worship? St. Paul wrote of "...the mystery hidden from ages and from generations past. But now... manifested to his holy ones, to whom God chose to make known the riches of the glory of this mystery among the Gentiles; it is Christ in you, the hope of glory" (Col 1:24-27). It is clear that St. Paul is not talking here about the Liturgy, but about God's entire plan for our salvation: all His love for us, from the day He freed His people Israel from the Egyptian tyranny culminating in our own day when He dwells in us as a pledge of the future kingdom.

Christ dwelling in us is the mystery and at the Liturgy Christ is in us in Communion. In one sense the mystery has been revealed! The "puzzle" has been solved! We see where the "clues" have been leading. There were clues in the Old Testament. Adam and Eve were driven from the tree of life, but the tree of life points to the cross, the wood on which Christ died. Eating of His body and blood we eat of the tree of life, "for God loved the world so much that he gave his only Son, so that whoever believes in him might not perish but might have everlasting life" (John 3:16). We have seen Abraham take his only son, Isaac to be sacrificed on the mountain, but how God accepted his faith and replaced Isaac with a lamb. Now the Father has sacrificed His only Son on the cross. Like Isaac, He carried the wood for the sacrifice, and His death was accepted by the Father as faith that brings life. Christ is the "Lamb of God," the *ahnec* (Slavonic for "lamb") of which we partake in Holy Communion.

We have seen how Moses freed the people of Israel in the Passover, when the angel of the Lord passed over the first-born children of Israel and struck down the first-born of Egypt, because the blood of the Paschal Lamb had been spread on the lintels of the doors of the Hebrew people. In the wood of the door we see a hint of the wood of the cross, now smeared with the blood of Jesus, the only Son of the Father. Jesus is the Paschal Lamb, who at the Passover supper gave us His body as food, and who was sacrificed on the cross while the Passover lambs were being slain in the temple.

The Old Testament is filled with clues to the mystery of Christ. We could mention the hints of baptism: the ark of Noah, the dividing of the Red Sea and the crossing of the Jordan. We could cite the figures of the resurrection: the raising of the Shunammite woman's son by Eliseus or the story of Jonah. What a tremendous and fascinating mystery — but a mystery has been solved. Humanity again has access to the tree of life in paradise, which now is the cross, and by Christ's blood we are all saved. This is called the Paschal, or Passover mystery. It is not obscure, but perfectly clear. By His death for others, Christ has led us into new life. He has done this absolutely, because in Him obedience to God destroyed by Adam's sin was restored.

There is another aspect of mystery in the Divine Liturgy but now it emerges through our understanding! The Liturgy is mystery because its deepest reality is hidden from ordinary sight and revealed only to eyes of faith as Chrysostom told us: "It is called mystery when we do not consider what we see [with our bodily eyes], but see one set of things and consider another... here the judgment of the believer is one thing, while that of the unbeliever is another. For myself, I hear that Christ has been crucified, and I at once marvel at His love for us; he who does not believe hears the same thing said and thinks that it is folly. The unbeliever, hearing of a bath [of baptism], thinks it is only water; I, on the other hand, consider not only what is seen, but the purification of the soul by the Holy Spirit" (Homily on 1 Corinthians 1, n. 7). Here again we see that our faith is a new way of seeing the world, and that the Liturgy leads us into new light.

There is a third dimension of mystery in what we believe and celebrate. While Christ's message is crystal clear, it is still a paradox! Life is found through death, only by loving our enemies and by losing our lives, can we find life! Jesus did this by way of example at the Last Supper. He washed His disciples' feet, telling them, "I have given you a model to follow, so that as I have done for you, you should also do" (John 13:15). The Liturgy, therefore, is both a memorial and model that we also should be ready to lay down our lives for others. "What greater love has anyone than to lay down his life for a friend?" (John 15:13) and "A new commandment I give to you, that you love one another as I have loved you" (John 13:34).

The mystery here is that we understand clearly that this must be so, but still wonder how it is so. Any doubts that it might not be so are demolished by the glorious resurrection of our Lord and God and Savior Jesus Christ. No one expressed this paradox better than St. Paul: "The message of the cross is foolishness to those who are perishing, but to us who are being saved it is the power of God. ... for Jews demand signs and Greeks look for wisdom, but we proclaim Christ crucified, a stumbling block to Jews and foolishness to Gentiles, but to those who are called, Jews and Greeks alike, Christ the power of God and the wisdom of God" (1 Corinthians 1:18.22-24).

Worship and a Sense of Awe

The deacon invites us to listen to the priest pray the anaphora, saying: "Let us stand aright, let us stand in awe..." Unfortunately, the word "awe" has been trivialized in slang with phrases like "Totally awesome!" True awe, however, leaves us speechless and amazed. As St. John Chrysostom said, "When the priest stands before the table, stretching forth his hands to heaven, calling on the Holy Spirit to be present, and to touch the oblations, there is a great stillness, a great silence" (*De coemet. appel. 3*).

When we realize the depth of the mystery in the Liturgy, we experience a sense of awe. We perceive the mystery with our intellect, but experience a sense of "awe" in our emotions. We need to understand the mystery, but our response to this understanding is awe. Without this sense of respect, awe, wonderment or reverence, then the Liturgy has no effect on us and becomes only a silly game. Abraham Heschel said, "Awe precedes faith," but we can add, "without awe there simply is no faith." If we don't have this interior attitude of respect and wonder and love, then the Liturgy becomes merely something to get over with as quickly as possible.

Jesus said, "Unless you become like little children, you cannot enter the kingdom of heaven." It is characteristic of children that they find the whole world amazing and wonderful. Children take very little that we as adults take for granted and every day for the child is filled with new discoveries. Indeed, children often find things amazing and wonderful that adults really wish they would not find so intriguing.

New Christians have often been described as "babes in Christ." Our Lord tells us, "Unless you are born again of water and the Spirit, you cannot enter the kingdom of heaven." The Church has always made this rebirth in baptism an "awe-inspiring rite of initiation." One of the reasons the Church grew was because faith was awesome and challenging. In the early centuries, in order to become a Christian, you had to go through several years of preparation. This required not only learning about the faith, but practicing it by charity towards others (community service) and by self-denial, especially fasting. The Church leaders wondered, "How can we give these new converts a sense of respect for their new faith?" They came up with a process of initiation for adults coming to baptism that was designed to inspire a sense of awe. The catechumenate, as this process was called, revolved around the "discipline of the secret." Before baptism the catechumens (learners) could only attend the teaching part of the Liturgy and were excluded from the prayers and the Eucharist. They were dismissed after the Gospel and homily, when the deacon exclaimed, "All catechumens, depart! Let none of the catechumens remain."

The catechumens could not participate in the mysteries. They could not address God as "Father." They could not receive the body of Christ, they could not drink of the Source of immortality! Then in one night, usually the eve of Pascha, the feast of the Lord's Resurrection, they were initiated. They went down into the water in baptism, and experienced what St. Paul had described, "We were indeed buried with him through baptism into death, so that just as Christ was raised from the dead by the glory of the Father, we too might live in newness of life" (Romans 6:4). Robed in white garments they took part in the Eucharistic sacrifice, and then they saw, they understood, they were enlightened. St John Chrysostom almost sings his explanation to the newly-baptized of what has happened to them:

> "Blessed be God, who alone does wonderful things, who does all things and transforms them. Before yesterday you were captives, but now you are free and citizens of the Church; lately you lived in the shame of your sins, but now you live in freedom and justice. You are not only free, but also holy; not only holy, but also just; not only just, but also sons; not only sons, but also heirs; not only heirs, but also brothers of Christ; not only brothers of Christ, but also joint

heirs; not only joint heirs, but also members; not only members, but also the temple; not only the temple, but also instruments of the Spirit! Blessed be God, who alone does wonderful things" (The Third Instruction, 5-6).

The Church has nothing to hide. It is not a secret society; it has always been open and public. However, just knowing what the Gospel is about, and experiencing it are different. The catechumenate was a program designed to make the participants experience what the faith really meant. We do the same today with in the Great Fast, when we pray and fast and do works of charity — so that we can experience annually what the catechumens experienced at their baptism. At resurrection matins, then, we can rightfully sing, "I was buried yesterday with You, O Christ, but today I rise, resurrected with You. Yesterday I was crucified with You, O Savior; now glorify me with You in Your kingdom."

In every Liturgy, we try to recreate this experience of awe. In the Old Testament the prophet Isaiah was struck with awe when he beheld the heavenly court (see Isaiah 6:1-3).   In the Liturgy we stand in the place of the angels: "Let us who mystically represent the Cherubim, and sing the thrice-holy hymn to the life-creating Trinity..." The cynical might say, isn't this just some kind of hype? But the Liturgy really is awesome, because here we are face to face with God and what we do is really beyond the angelic powers: Again we can quote John Chrysostom, "O, what a marvel! What love of God to humanity! He who sits on high with the Father is at that hour held in the hands of all, and gives Himself to those who are willing to grasp and embrace Him. And all do this through the eyes of faith!" (*On the Priesthood* 3,4) It is the eyes of faith that are important. Through these eyes we see something new and awesome.

Modern popularizers of science try to see the universe in a new way when they humble the human species by speaking about the "billions and billions and billions" of galaxies. We Christians just take this awe one step further and view the universe with eyes of faith when we sing, "Holy, holy, holy, Lord of hosts, heaven and earth are full of your glory."   In this tremendous universe of billions and billions and billions of galaxies, in which we might seem to appear as insignificant motes, we alone can stand and praise the Creator of all who has given Himself to us. Indeed, how can we not believe His promise of everlasting life? It is the Spirit that gives life, and in the Liturgy we see everything with the eyes of the Spirit.

Tradition and the Liturgy

Tradition is a word that we all recognize, but which can mean many different things. Of all the words of religion, however, tradition is most important, and we change tradition at our peril. First of all, though, we must distinguish between the Tradition and traditionalism. The Tradition is real and alive. It is our direct link with Christ. Through the Tradition we experience directly the reality that is His life. The intervening centuries between His time and ours fade away into nothing. We experience Christ as present with us here. Traditionalism, however, is hanging on to meaningless and dead customs for no reason other than "that's what we've always done," and we have no more understanding or even desire to know what these customs mean. As the well-known Orthodox theologian Jaroslav Pelikan said, "Tradition is the living faith of the dead; traditionalism is the dead faith of the living."

Tradition means "that which is handed on" and is especially concerned with our liturgical worship. The Liturgy is a primary experience of the Tradition, as St. Paul observes, "For I received from the Lord what I also handed on to you, that the Lord Jesus, on the night He was handed over, took bread, and, after He had given thanks, broke it and said, 'This is my body that is for you. Do this in remembrance of me.' In the same way also the cup, after supper, saying, 'This cup is the new covenant in my blood. Do this, as often as you drink it, in remembrance of me.' For as often as you eat this bread and drink the cup, you proclaim the death of the Lord until He comes" (1 Corinthians 11:23-26).

The Tradition is not simply what we remember our grandparents doing; it is Christ's message of salvation that is necessary for life. Each generation must discover it anew. This is very difficult for this generation because we live in an age which has suffered a break with its past. It is an age in which people think that anything over twenty years old — including people — is old-fashioned, obsolete and to be thrown out. It is also important for us to understand what the Tradition is and to value it, because we have also made many errors about what it is.

The Tradition is different from custom. Customs are the concrete things that we do, such as bless food on Pascha, or remember the dead on Saturdays in the Great Fast, or sing ten stichera at Psalm 140 for Sunday Vespers. Customs change, and it is possible to establish a "contrary custom," by doing something for a certain number of years, but the Tradition does not change. The Tradition is what has been handed down from Christ. Tradition is less the concrete, distinct customs than the innermost reality that gives them life and meaning. Whatever is only found in a book — be it the Bible or a liturgikon — is dead, unless it is seen with a living eye. The Tradition is the living memory of what it means to be a Christian. The Divine Liturgy is such a living memory, which unites us to what happened two thousand years ago. At the mystical supper, the Gospel tells us, Jesus "took bread, said the blessing, broke it and gave it to His disciples," and we do the same: we take bread at the great entrance; we bless it at the anaphora; we break it at the fraction; we give it in Holy Communion.

In the Tradition we see that the Liturgy presumes love of one another. In our Liturgy today the deacon invites us, "let us love one another" before the Creed. While the customs of the giving of peace and forgiveness have varied throughout history, yet they express the living Tradition as our Lord commanded, "If you bring your gifts to the altar, and there recall that your brother has anything against you, go first and be reconciled with your brother, and then come and offer your gift" (Matthew 5:23-24). It is living Tradition that we bless the gifts in the anaphora as our Lord did. It is the living Tradition that tells us that the Liturgy is completed by Communion. The priest cannot celebrate a Liturgy without receiving Communion, though at times the laity has forgotten, that our Lord said, "Drink of this, all of you."

Every historic Church does these things. They are more than mere customs, they are the Tradition: the memorial of Jesus Christ, which is expressed in different ways in different Churches. Sometimes, unfortunately, particularly in the modern age, some of the most important expressions of this Tradition have been reduced too much, and we need to rediscover them, especially the meaning of the anaphora.

Despite the fact that the Tradition is not a body of concrete and distinct customs, this does not mean that it is vague. It is really very clear and exact. It may be expressed in different ways. In fact, it must be expressed in different ways and in different languages if it is to be a real "handing down." Even within the same culture and language, words and ways of expression change their meaning from generation to generation. What meant one thing to our grandparents may mean something entirely different to our grandchildren. I speak here not only of words, but of ways of life, of preconceptions and of the differences in environment. As we make technological progress, and change the world, our customs must change precisely that the Tradition might stay the same. And so the universal Church warns our particular Church, "You must return to your ancestral traditions," and develop them only "in an organic way."

We must avoid "traditionalism" like a plague, for a mindless clinging to what has been done can distort and ruin the Tradition, but we must be true "traditionalists," people who work to understand the faith and to celebrate it with beauty. Tradition remembers the past, but the past is our future and true, living Tradition always looks confidently to the future. The final prayer in the Liturgy of St. Basil illustrates this aspect of the Tradition. "The mystery of your plan, O Christ our God, has been completed and perfected as far as it was in our power. We have commemorated your death; we have seen the figure of your resurrection; we have been filled with your unending life; we have enjoyed your inexhaustible delights. Grant that we be made worthy of all this in the world to come through the grace of your eternal Father and of your good and life-creating Spirit."

The Liturgy as Sacrifice

When, as young people of the last generation, we learned our catechism, the most common word used to describe the Divine Liturgy was "sacrifice." This was very much a part of our Catholic identity, as defined in the Council of Trent. The word "sacrifice" remains always one of the most important in our faith. There can be no doubt that the Divine Liturgy is a sacrifice; and even ancient texts of the Divine Liturgy describe this mystery as a sacrifice. In fact, the proper word for the Eucharistic prayer is the anaphora, the "prayer of offering" and it is exactly sacrifices that are "offered." As one of the hymns from Holy Wednesday says, "He who wrote the tables of the Law on Sinai, Himself fulfilled the ordinance of the Law. He ate the old Passover which was but a shadow, and He became the new Passover, a mystical and living sacrifice" (8th Ode, Matins).

However, the word sacrifice is not popular in some circles, perhaps because we've misunderstood it in two ways. These two ways of misunderstanding are connected. First there is the problem of equating Christ's sacrifice with merely one part of it: His death on the cross. In the Old Testament a sacrifice involved three parts: the killing of the lamb or ram, it's offering to God by the priest and the eating of what had been offered by priest and people. Since we often think of "sacrifice" as the giving up of our lives or some portion of our lives, we consider Christ's sacrifice only as His death on the cross.

Christ, risen from the dead, ascended to His Father to offer the sacrifice which had been slain. The Epistle to the Hebrews describes this in liturgical terms:

> "He entered once for all into the Holy Place, taking not the blood of goats and calves but his own blood, thus securing an eternal redemption. ... For Christ has entered, not into a sanctuary made with hands, a copy of the true one, but into heaven itself, now to appear in the presence of God on our behalf. Nor was it to offer himself repeatedly, as the high priest enters the Holy Place yearly with blood not his own;

for then he would have had to suffer repeatedly since the foundation of the world. But as it is, he has appeared once for all at the end of the age to put away sin by the sacrifice of himself" (Hebrews 9:12, 24-26).

The sacrifice in the Liturgy is our participation in this Paschal mystery of death and life, of the cross and the resurrection. When we restrict the sacrifice to the death of Christ, we miss seeing what the cross truly represents. Every Sunday and all during Paschaltime we pray at Matins, "Let us adore Christ's holy resurrection, for, behold, through the cross joy has come into the whole world." On the Sunday of the Veneration of the Cross, we sing the kontakion, "No longer does the flaming sword guard the gates of Eden, for on them one finds the most glorious seal, the tree of the cross. By it the sorrow of death and the victory of the Abyss have been conquered. For you, O my Savior, stood and called out to those in the Abyss, 'Enter again into paradise.'" Christ's sacrifice includes not only death, but also life and resurrection.

This is why the offering is such an important moment in the Liturgy. The priest prays, "Remembering, therefore, this salutary command, and all that was done in our behalf: the cross, the tomb, the resurrection on the third day, the ascension into heaven, the sitting at the right hand, the second and glorious coming again, ...we offer to you [the Father] yours of your own," His only Son, who is our peace. There is now only one true priest, and one true sacrifice: the offering of Jesus the High Priest. The Divine Liturgy is our sharing in this one sacrifice.

The third part of the sacrifice occurs when we receive Communion, when we partake of God, and we become united in fellowship in Christ, the One who offered and who is offered. There can be no Liturgy without Communion, because a sacrifice includes communion, a sharing in the fruit of the sacrifice. In the Old Testament, we see very clearly that it was the worshipper's desire for intimacy with God that made sacrifices acceptable to God.

Intimacy with God is possible only in Christ. In the Garden of paradise, Adam and Eve had walked with God and were His close friends, but lost this by sin. We also had the gift of immortality, but this was also lost by sin. We desperately wanted to regain this friendship with God. How could this be done? Adam and Eve had been disobedient. Could we, by our obedience, regain paradise? How could we show restore communion with Him?

The only way we could regain God's friendship was by losing everything — our whole lives — as Jesus was to point out, "no greater love has anyone than to lay down his life for a friend" (John 15:13). For us, this was impossible, because, by God's very command, we were only stewards of our lives, which belonged to God the Creator. We tried, then, to appease God by animal sacrifices as if we were saying, "Look, this is what we want, we want to give everything to you, but we can't, so please accept these tokens."

The Epistle to the Hebrews again puts its finger on the problem: "But in those sacrifices there is only a yearly remembrance of sins, for it is impossible that the blood of bulls and goats take away sins." (10: 3-4) God solved this problem by becoming human Himself. Then, one Person could offer Himself completely in sacrifice, yet not be destroyed; He could be perfectly obedient to the Father and offer everything to the Father, and yet give life through the resurrection. Jesus, therefore, showed us very clearly that "whoever saves his life will lose it, but whoever loses his life for my sake and for the Gospel's sake will find it" (Mark 8:35). He found life for all humanity by losing His life on the cross. St. Paul said, "For he is our peace, he who made both one and broke down the dividing wall of enmity" (Ephesians 2:14).

Two further notes: The Liturgy is described as a "spiritual and unbloody sacrifice..." In fact, we do not find the word "sacrifice" unless it is qualified as a "spiritual," or "unbloody," or "liturgical" sacrifice. In his prayer during the Cherubikon, the priest asks Christ to make him worthy to celebrate the Liturgy, because the Lord Jesus is the one who "gave into our keeping the holy office of this liturgical, unbloody sacrifice." There does not have to be any material re-enactment of the death of Christ who died once for all.

The Liturgy is also called "a sacrifice of praise." Our praise of God becomes a real, living sacrifice there is a spirit of sacrifice in it. Our desire to give ourselves completely to God is joined to that of Christ, who has given himself completely to the Father, because He has become one of us uniting the divine and human. St. Paul therefore could write: "I urge you, therefore, brothers, by the mercies of God, to offer your bodies as a living sacrifice, holy and pleasing to God, your spiritual worship" (Romans 12:3).

The Liturgy as Union with God

Communion is the final goal of the Liturgy, which is not complete until we receive the body and blood of Christ. Then everything is changed. There is no more penance or fasting. The prayers, which before asked God to make us worthy, now thank Him for having made us worthy. In the first Prayer of the Faithful, for example, the priest says silently, "Accept our prayer, O God, and make us worthy to offer to you prayers and supplications, and unbloody sacrifices for all your people." However, after Holy Communion, the priest prays aloud in the Prayer of Thanksgiving, "We thank you, O Master, Benefactor of our souls, who love us all, that this day you have made us worthy of your heavenly and immortal mysteries."

After Communion, we are a new person. We are deified. We are now worthy of God: "We have seen the true light." We are enlightened: "We have received the heavenly Spirit." We are christened. We are now the Body of Christ and, therefore, we are all equal. Communion is the primary democracy, for no one can receive more or less of Christ. This is the teaching of St. John Chrysostom:

> "All things are equal between us and you, even the very chief of our blessings. I do not partake of the Holy Table with greater abundance and you with less, but both equally partake of the same. And if I take it first, this is no great privilege, since even among children, the elder first extends his hand to the feast, and no advantage is gained in this way. But with us all things are equal. The saving life that

sustains our souls is given with equal honor to both. I do not indeed partake of one Lamb and you of another, but we partake of the same. We both have the same baptism. We have been given the same Spirit. We are both hastening to the same kingdom. We are alike brethren of Christ, we have all things in common" (Fourth Homily on 1 Thessalonians).

We must have humility both before and after Communion. Humility before: because we are unworthy of union with Christ. We approach Him as sinners and we confess, "O Lord, be merciful to me, a sinner." Humility after: because we are in union with Christ and through Him with one another. Through Communion with Christ we are called to that service to one another that Christ showed at the Last Supper when He washed the feet of His disciples. This is imitation of Christ, who was "meek and humble of heart," (Matthew 11:29) obedient to His Father unto death on the cross. This is what St. Paul means when he writes, "Have among yourselves the same attitude that is also yours in Christ Jesus." (Philippians 2:5)

Humility is almost a forgotten virtue in the kind of world that we live in today, where it is often mistaken for "weakness," and "groveling." This is a prejudice from a consumer society that teaches us to pamper ourselves, to give ourselves what we "deserve" and to stand up for what is "due to us." Our whole lives can become preoccupied with what we have and what we do. We live in an individualistic society where rugged individualism is praised and bending to the needs of others is not.

Humility could be better described as true realism. After all, when Adam sinned, God spoke quite harshly to him: "You are dirt, and to dirt you shall return" (Genesis 3:19). The humble person, then, is realistic, having his feet on the ground. If we really know ourselves in humility, then we can hear God's saving words, "Whoever exalts himself will be humbled, but whoever humbles himself will be exalted" (Matthew 23:12).

In Communion we come to God as we are; and as we eat of the products of the earth — grapes which grow from the ground and bread made from wheat which grows from the ground — our humility is united with the Creator of all, who has made that bread and wine His body and blood. Jesus is "the very imprint of his Father's being" (Hebrews 1:3). When we receive Him in Holy Communion, we become what we eat: Jesus, the Word of God. John speaks very realistically about eating God. "Just as the living Father sent me and I have life because of the Father, so also the one who feeds on me will have life because of me" (John 6:57). Many of Jesus' followers left Him, "This saying is hard; who can accept it?" (John 6:60) We must notice carefully what Jesus says, "Everyone who listens to my Father and learns from him comes to me... I am the bread of life" (John 6:45.48), "I am the way, the truth and the life" (John 14:6). To partake of the Eucharist is to commit ourselves to Christ, and to keep His commandments. On Holy Thursday we sing, "Come, you faithful, let us with uplifted mind enjoy the hospitality and the immortal banquet of the Lord; for we have learned exalted words from the Word who has ascended, and whom we glorify" (Ninth Ode, Holy Thursday matins).

In Communion, we eat what seems to the unbelieving eye as only a little bread and wine, but we are truly united with God, one in the Holy Trinity. Our union with God is physical, for we partake of His body and blood. It is mental, for our minds are enlightened with new understanding. It is spiritual, for we are lifted into life in the Trinity. We become one with God and one in God to form a new community, as His Church, His people, and His priesthood. Therefore, in the prayer at the consummation of the gifts, which concludes the Liturgy, we affirm: "You, O Christ, our God, who are the fulfillment of the law and the prophets, have fulfilled the whole plan of the Father; fill our hearts with joy and gladness, always, now and ever and forever."

Love for the Liturgy

There can be no doubt that the Divine Liturgy is the center of the life of a parish community. It is the place where the people come together in the greatest numbers. In any parish there may be social events and organization meetings and catechesis both of adults and children, but not everyone will take part in all these events.   One cannot be a real member of the parish, however, without attending the Liturgy.

As far as I know, no one has done a really in-depth study of why people attend the Liturgy.   It would be very difficult to do this. Many people would find it hard to express why they go to church; while, for others, it may be a very personal question with uncomfortable answers.   Therefore, out of my experience in cele-brating the Liturgy, in feeling peoples' response, and in talking with them, I have to make some guesses.

Today we have many attitudes regarding the Liturgy.   Some people find it gives them the energy they need for life; others find it a comforting and reassuringly stable influence on their journey through life, while still others attend out of duty and find it boring and irrelevant.

There is no doubt that some people attend the Liturgy because it is the law.   The Church's law is that we must attend the Divine Liturgy on Sunday and some holy days.   A legalistic motive is clear when people seek out the shortest Liturgy or ask how much of the Liturgy they must attend.   They are asking, "What is the least I have to do to fulfill the law?"   Fifty years ago, this legal motive was much more prevalent.   In today's world, legal religious demands are less important.   Only a minority wants no more than the legal limit, while others have become "cultural Catholics" and do not feel obliged to attend Liturgy at all to maintain their status as members.   For them, Church law does not have the power it once did

The Liturgy will not be meaningful to us unless it is frequented for its own sake, on account of its authentic meaning.   Whenever motives other than the worship of God are applied, they always destroy the character of the worship.   If we go to church only because it is the law, then our worship becomes lifeless for us.   It is not that the law is bad, because it is a guideline to what we should be doing as Christians, but that it is not being observed in spirit.

Another reason often presented for attending church is that it gives people a particular identity.   When people say that the most important purpose of the Liturgy is to affirm their identity, they are likely to give more importance to external elements such as particular gestures or the language used. When the Liturgy becomes only a badge of identity, its deeper meaning fades, and some aspects of it — such as the words of our prayers and hymns — become unimportant. However, if we celebrate the Liturgy only because it is part of our identity — particularly an ethnic identity — then it does not give us life, because this is only external. Perhaps this is the reason why our worship was conducted in a dead language for so many centuries: its real meaning was not important to us. Liturgy is life-giving only when it brings us into communion with God, and this implies understanding, at least as much as possible for our limited human intelligence, for God will always remains a mystery.

Answering the question, "Why should we attend the Liturgy?" becomes possible only if we ask some even more fundamental questions. Why are we alive? How do we relate to God? What do we think of Him? Struggling to comprehend Him with our limited human intelligence and imagination, we sometimes tend to view Him as an absolute, all-powerful and jealous — albeit somewhat benevolent — tyrant. For many people, therefore, worship just becomes one more unreasonable demand of this very arrogant personage. As believers, this is probably not our opinion of God, but it has to be admitted that this image influences us.

Any concepts of God we come up with are necessarily inadequate, because as finite beings, we cannot grasp God. This is why we pray in the Liturgy, "You are God ineffable, inconceivable, invisible, incomprehensible." We cannot speak of God as "jealous" or "tyrannical," because we exist only in His creating, sustaining and loving word. He is Goodness who has brought us freely out of non-existence into being. As the wise Syrian theologian who wrote under the name of Dionysius taught, "No words can come up to the inexpressible Good, this One, the Source of all unity, this supra-existent Being, mind beyond mind, words beyond speech, it is gathered up by no discourse, by no intuition, by no name. It is and it is as no other being is" (*Divine Names* 1,1).

Western culture today is strongly humanist, if we mean by this that "humans," as the crown of creation, create by themselves the meaning of human life. In our daily activities, our needs become the priority. We find it easy to turn reality on its head and ask what God owes us, rather than how we should relate to Him. Worship of God is simply another burden, and one that does not seem to make sense at times. Worship of God may even be seen as demeaning to the human person, therefore Liturgy becomes useless or even is seen to manifest an infantile attitude on our part towards God.

But as human beings we cannot change the nature of reality. God has given us everything that we have and has made us everything that we are. Even those who deny that there is a God live and move and have their being in Him. And so to exist without worship is like trying to breathe without air. Worship is life. When we consciously glorify God and pray to Him for our needs, we are most alive in Him, and touch the very Cause of our being. We all must do this, even though in many times and places people have substituted false ideas of God in place of truth.

In all of this, Christian worship and, in particular, the Divine Liturgy has a particular place. In the entertainment media, God is often presented as one person much like others, as in the George Burns "Oh God" films, or Jim Carrey's more recent movie, *Bruce Almighty*. In our history, however, only one Person has been identified as God: Jesus, the Son and Word of God. After His resurrection, Thomas professed Him, "My Lord and my God." At the Last Supper, Jesus told Philip, "Whoever has seen me has seen the Father"(John 14:9), and the author of the Epistle to the Hebrews proclaims Him as "the refulgence of [God's] glory, the very imprint of his being, who sustains all things by his mighty word" (Hebrews 1:1). Jesus is the revelation of God to us, though we have not yet completely understood Him, and in Him all thing are sustained. Therefore, He is not one like the others, but the One in whom "we live and move and have our being." (Acts 17:28).

In Christ we see the "very imprint of God's being" and it is He who has asked this particular form of worship of us, as He told His disciples at the Last Supper, "Do this in memory of me." One might object that if we celebrate the Liturgy because our Lord commanded it, then we are still only worshiping because of external reasons. However, divine law is different from human law. God does not give us external and arbitrary directives. His law is less an imposition than a revelation. Therefore, if God says, "do not kill," "do not commit adultery," "do not lie," "do not steal," it is because if we do these things we are no longer the creatures He intended us to be. We have "died in sin," and become less than human.

When Christ says, "Do this in memory of me," He is calling on us to recognize His desire to be consciously present to us, giving us divine life in Holy Communion. When we receive Communion in the holy body and precious blood of our Lord, Jesus Christ, Son and Word of God, we are united in our whole being, body, mind and soul, with the "ineffable, inconceivable, invisible and incomprehensible God."

The Liturgy is essential, and my conviction is that the Byzantine Liturgy is the highest expression of Christian worship. Yet despite all, this, many still find worship "boring." If our Church is to survive (God has guaranteed that the Church will survive, but not necessarily all the particular Churches within the universal community of faith), then we must try to understand the meaning of our Liturgy and how it can express the very essence of our life and faith. I hope in subsequent chapters to explore the different sections of the Liturgy and reflect on the meaning of each one.

For Your Reflection

1. Worship is traditionally seen as the true fulfillment of our nature. Why might some people find it demeaning?

2. Prayer gestures are wordless ways of expressing aspects of the mystery of God. What are some gestures used in our worship and what aspect of God do you believe these gestures express?

3. What are the three aspects of a sacrifice mentioned in this chapter and how do we experience them in the Divine Liturgy?

Chapter Two — Preparation, Assembly and Catechetical Rites

The celebration of the Divine Liturgy is not a ritual irrelevant to life. It touches how we live, raising us as living beings having body and soul to participate as much as we are able, in the life of God. For this reason, when we gather to celebrate the Divine Liturgy, we do not simply step over some absolute boundary that keeps our worship in the church isolated from our daily concerns. It is true that at the great entrance, we sing, "Let us set aside all earthly cares, that we may welcome the King of all." However, this indicates a difficulty of translation. In English, "earthly cares" is more general, but the hymn here is quoting directly from the Gospel of St. Luke (8:14), where the seed of the gospel of Jesus Christ is "choked by the anxieties and riches and pleasures of life," and fails to produce fruit. The "earthly cares" we must set aside are those "anxieties" that would keep us from keeping the word of God. If all this is so, then when we approach the Divine Liturgy, we must go through some private preparation to go from the individual lives we lead in the world to the community of God's people in the "Kingdom of the Father, and of the Son and of the Holy Spirit."

How should we prepare for the Divine Liturgy? In a way, our preparation is like a small Lent, because each celebration of the Eucharist is a commemoration of the mystery of Pascha, the death and resurrection of our Lord. We prepare for Pascha by prayer, fasting and almsgiving. The Church has prescribed prayers to be said before the Divine Liturgy. Some of these prayers will be included in the books that are intended for the use of the people attending the Liturgy. If we arrive at the church early enough, we may say some of these prayers to ourselves.

45

The Church prescribes the public praying of the Third Hour before the Liturgy, but this practice has all but disappeared in our parishes, and has been replaced by various popular hymns. The purpose of these prayers is to serve as a transition to a new reality, our entrance into God's presence in the holy mysteries.

A second way of preparation is through fasting. The more traditional custom is to abstain from food from rising to the reception of Holy Communion. Therefore, our bodies are sanctified at the start of the day by receiving the body and blood of Christ. To encourage more frequent reception of Communion, the Church has mitigated the fasting requirement to one hour before Holy Communion. This is important for people who would suffer physical hardship if they were unable to eat regularly, as, for example, diabetics. If we are able, though, it would be good to keep a stricter fast.

While we need not give alms, that is, donate money to the poor, before the Liturgy, we should approach each Liturgy in a spirit of charity. We cannot enter the church with hatred in our heart for any of God's creatures. This may require us at times to seek reconciliation with another, or to perform works of mercy for others before the Liturgy, while our whole lives must be lived in a Christian spirit.

Prayers before the Doors

There is a formal preparation prescribed by the Church for the priest and deacon. This preparation involves their personal prayer and then the preparation of the gifts of bread and wine for the Liturgy. As the priest and deacon step from the world into the church, and specifically into the altar, there is a series of prayers said before the icon screen. These consist of the normal beginning prayers, the general troparia for needs, and then a troparion before the icon of our Lord and another before the icon of the Mother of God. The priest and deacon do not enter the holy space without making themselves aware of the presence of our Lord, who, after His resurrection, promised to be with us always (Matthew 28:20) and of the saints, as the Epistle to the Hebrews reminds us, "since we are surrounded by so great a cloud of witnesses, let us rid ourselves of every burden and sin that clings to us" (Hebrews 12:1). No human being can accomplish that on his own, and so the priest prays for God's grace: "Lord, stretch forth your hand from the height of your holy dwelling-place, and strengthen me for the service I am about to offer you that I may stand before your awesome altar without condemnation and perform the unbloody sacrifice. For yours is the power forever. Amen."

Only God can possibly allow the priest to celebrate these mysteries, as St. John Chrysostom taught, "The work of the priesthood is done on earth, but it is ranked among heavenly ordinances. ... The priest, therefore, must be as pure as if he were standing in heaven itself, in the midst of those powers [the angels]" (*On the Priesthood* 3:4).

Preparation of the Gifts

The priest and deacon also prepare the bread and wine to be used in the Divine Liturgy. Originally, the faithful donated the gifts for liturgical use. Indeed, in many parishes today, the parishioners still bake the bread for the Liturgy. The deacon would choose the best loaf of bread and would place it on the diskos, the plate that held the gifts about to be offered, a responsibility that was transferred to the priest as the rite of preparation developed. In this way, we see that not only people, but also the material elements to be offered must make a passage from the ordinary world into the realm of God's mysteries. The bread and wine that are chosen are destined to become instruments of our sanctification as we eat and drink of the body and blood of our Lord.

At the same time, this rite is accompanied by commemoration of the saints, of our departed brothers and sisters in faith, and of the living members of the Church, the Body of Christ (see Ephesians 1:22-23) who are in need of our love and our prayers. The priest then prays, "God, O God... bless these gifts placed here before you and accept them on your heavenly altar. Remember, as the merciful Lover of Mankind, those who brought the offerings and those for whom they are being offered; and keep us blameless in the holy celebration of your divine mysteries."

The Great Incensation

The Divine Liturgy begins publicly when the deacon (or priest, if there is no deacon) incenses the entire church. In ancient times, the censer was not swung, but was carried in a hand-held container. However, the swinging censer became much more popular as a more efficient way of spreading the fragrance of the incense. The altar, the "holy of holies," is censed first, then the nave, the interior of the church, and finally the people. As he censes, the deacon says to himself Psalm 50, which gives us the meaning of this ritual action: "O purify me, then I shall be clean ... Then you will be pleased with lawful sacrifices" (Psalm 50:9, 21). The incensation spreads a sweet smell in the church, purifying the altar, the meeting place of the church, and the assembly, so that the sacrifice of the Liturgy may be offered worthily.

Today, many people criticize the use of incense. Sometimes this comes from a purely interior approach to divine worship. In the Eastern Liturgy, God is to be worshiped with our whole being, and, therefore, all of our senses — sight, taste, hearing and even smell — are affected. Because of the incarnation — the doctrine that God has become flesh — we, who are creatures of spirit and matter, have been sanctified, and matter itself is made fit for worship.

Of course, today there is another problem with incense. Some people, a small minority, do become overly sensitive to incense. While their needs must be taken into consideration, we must remember that allergenic substances are not taken out of use but are regulated. So, too, to abolish incense would remove one of the richest symbols of our Liturgy. As we shall see, it not only signifies purification and hence forgiveness, but also the presence of the Spirit, who surrounded Christ as a cloud on Mount Tabor, and of the action of Christ, who makes us "a sacrificial offering to God for a fragrant aroma" (Ephesians 5:2).

The Opening Dialogue

When the deacon has finished incensing the church and the congregation, he asks the priest for the blessing to begin the Divine Liturgy. Our original translation of this first dialogue ("It is time to sacrifice to the Lord") was slightly in error, since no word for "sacrifice" appears in the original Greek. This verse is, instead, a quotation of Psalm 118:126. The deacon says to the priest, "It is time for the Lord to act."

The Psalm continues noting that, while the Lord is asked to act, the people have broken His law. The Liturgy, then, would seem to be a time of judgment. We are sinners, and the Lord must judge that sinfulness and take the necessary action. Every encounter with God, holy and good, deifying and transforming us, fascinating us with their mystery, is also fearful, for we are unworthy to enter the presence of God. Yet God continues to summon us more deeply into the mystery as, when He invites us to Holy Communion, the deacon will say, "Approach with the fear of God and with faith."

Here we begin to understand that the Liturgy is not simply a human activity, but is in truth an action of God. From this passage alone, we know that we are now to offer the Divine Liturgy, in which it is not only we who pray, but Christ prays in us, and the Spirit "Himself intercedes with inexpressible groanings," "for we do not know how to pray as we ought" (Romans 8:26).

"Father, Give the Blessing"

The deacon then leaves the altar and goes to his place on the solea. Here he says the first public words of the Divine Liturgy to begin this divine action, "Father, give the blessing." In the original texts, this invitation is addressed to the *despota* (Greek) or *vladyko* (Slavonic). The deacon is addressing the one who presides (bishop or priest), asking him to say the first blessing, "Blessed is the kingdom of the Father, and of the Son and of the Holy Spirit, now and ever and forever." While some have said that this invitation to bless is actually addressed to God, who alone is Master, this is not too likely and we must follow the more obvious meaning here.

Vladyko or *despota* was an ordinary title of respect for someone in a position of authority. That *vladyko* applies to human beings as well as God can be seen in the acclamation, *Na mnohaja lita, Vladyko*, ("For many years, O Master,") for you would hardly ask that God be granted "many years."

In contemporary English, we do not usually call men, "Master," which traditionally has been used for underage boys. Likewise, in earlier centuries, while the bishop would have been called "Master," there was no distinct title for secular priests who would often serve in the place of the bishop, which has become the more common practice. For the priest, then, the title "Father" was developed. This title was originally used for a monk, not for a secular priest, but it has become common now to call all priests "Father."

Yet Jesus said that we are only to call God, "Father" (Matthew 23:9). The wise spiritual theologian, Irenee Hausherr, explained this practice best. He wrote, "The Lord gave this explicit warning: 'You must call no one on earth your father, since you have only one Father, and he is in heaven.' If such prohibitions did not prevent certain very godly Christians from calling mere mortals 'Father' or 'Abba', it is because — far from viewing this habit as an act of disobedience to the Lord's admonition — they advisedly saw in it homage to the one fatherhood of God, just as we do not disregard the solemn declaration of Christ, 'There is one alone who is good,' when we recognize goodness in human beings. Created goodness praises the one source of all goodness." This is why, when a priest is asked for a blessing, he immediately defers it to the one who is the fount of all blessings. When we ask a priest, "Father, bless," and the priest answers, "Blessed is our God..." so, too, in the Liturgy, the blessing is given to God, specifically here to His kingdom among us.

The Opening Exclamation

The priest responds to the deacon's request by exclaiming, "Blessed is the Kingdom of the Father, and of the Son and of the Holy Spirit." The Gospel of our Lord Jesus Christ was concerned with the Kingdom of God. In His Sermon on the Mount, Jesus told His followers not to worry about food or drink, clothing or shelter. Because God loves us, He will provide for us, and so He commands us, "Seek first the kingdom of God and his righteousness, and all these things will be given you as well" (Matthew 6:33). From the very first moment of the Liturgy, our attention is focused on God's Kingdom, and, as we see, on His righteousness. We must enter the Liturgy with the right mind, our concern that the will of God be done.

The difficulty with religion, however, is determining what is the will of God. Many people seem to be quite convinced that the will of God is, very simply, the same thing that they want. This is one of the true pitfalls of faith, especially for those in service to the Church. It is too easy to confuse our own will with God's. Of course, it's a natural human impulse to think that we are right and that everyone else is wrong. Someone who lives with a sense of reality, however, is aware that he or she can make a mistake. Discernment of the will of God is only possible if we have the humility to know that we can be wrong and probably are. To "seek the kingdom of God" means to do the best we can, knowing that we are often wrong and that God will work through us anyhow despite our mistakes. When a man is ordained a deacon, priest or bishop, the first words of the ordaining bishop are, "God, who heals all illnesses and supplies what is lacking..." Humility is a necessary virtue to serve the Kingdom of God, whether as a layperson or as an ordained minister.

What can we say, though, about the Kingdom? The Gospels are full of the teachings of Jesus about God's Kingdom. When He was led before Pontius Pilate, Jesus made this important declaration: "My kingdom is not of this world" (John 18:36). God's Kingdom does not have armies or treasuries or an organization. There is a difference between the Church and the Kingdom of God. While the Church must have an outward organization, the Kingdom of God rules through the hearts of its members. This does not mean that the Church is not of the

Kingdom, only that it is simply a way by which the Kingdom manifests itself.

Because the Kingdom is not an organization, it is less a "thing" than a dynamic in the life of faith. Thus the word translated here in the Liturgy by "Kingdom" is more an action than a geographical place or an organized structure. We might better say, "Blessed is the reign of God among us..." but this is more awkward. The word "reign" might be misunderstood or confused for something else. When we say, "Blessed is the kingdom..." we are making a commitment to actively work, in humility and love, to bring about God's righteousness in our lives and in the world. We also recognize that the Kingdom is not yet fully realized, and the Liturgy reminds us that we are on the path to God's glory. St. Maximos the Confessor wrote that the Liturgy is "the revelation of the mystery of our salvation which is in the most secret recesses of the divine... as the Word of God says to His disciples, 'I shall not drink of the fruit of the vine until that day when I drink it anew with you in the kingdom of my Father...'" (*The Church's Mystagogy*, 16, quoting Matthew 26:29). Every Divine Liturgy is our carrying out in action what we pray frequently during the day, "Thy Kingdom come, Thy will be done."

The blessing of the Kingdom ends with the words, "now and ever and forever." These words occur frequently in the Divine Liturgy, at the end of every doxology. This translates the more literal, "unto ages of ages." The phrase, "forever and ever" was chosen by the first translators of our recension in 1964. At that time it was explained that "forever" meant the same thing as "ages of ages." The difficulty in translating this expression has been around for a long time. I think even the Mediaeval English sensed the difficulty and came up with the unusual "world without end." One author attaches the original meaning of "ages to ages" to the idea of human generations. Its original meaning was "human life-span after human lifespan," therefore either a very long time, or eternally, that is, without beginning or end. We have a limited life-span, but God is eternal, before any human was and beyond the life-span of any human. Most interpret "ages of ages" now to mean, "…beyond all created cycles into the now of eternity." My personal opinion is that both translations are acceptable.

However, we cannot confuse "ages" with complicated theories and speculations about the cyclic nature of creation. Scientifically, most don't believe in the nature of the universe as a series of cycles. It had a beginning, it will have an end, but God has no beginning and no end. While we are alive in space and time, we cannot form ideas of eternity. This can happen only when we die and enter eternity, freed from our "secular" existence, when we rise in the "spiritual body" (1 Corinthians 15:44). As St. Paul said, "At present we see indistinctly, as in a mirror, but then face to face" (1 Corinthians 13:12). The Kingdom of God, then, is in the eternity of God, and the Liturgy is our way to God's reign. It is our truth and our life.

The Litany of Peace

After the opening blessing, the Divine Liturgy continues with what is often called the litany of peace, though there is no official name for it. The first three petitions are for "peace." This goes back into our Jewish source of faith, where the common greeting when people met was *shalom*, ("Peace"). The Gospels record that when Jesus rose from the dead, He "came and stood in the midst [of His disciples] and said to them, 'Peace be with you'" (John 20:19). Every Liturgy is a celebration of the resurrection, and it has been the constant tradition of the Church that the Liturgy begins with a greeting of peace, in the name of "God with us." St. Paul tells us explicitly that Christ "is our peace, who made both [Jew and Gentile] one and broke down the dividing wall of enmity, through his flesh" (Ephesians 2:14). This happens in every Liturgy, as we become partakers of God's "holy, divine, immortal, pure, and life-creating mysteries" (hymn after Communion). In this celebration, Christ establishes peace, reconciling us "with God, in one body, through the cross, putting that enmity to death by it" (Ephesians 2:16).

The Liturgy did not begin originally with the litany of peace. It was first said after the catechumens (unbaptized learners) and the penitents were dismissed. It began the part of the Liturgy meant for the faithful who were going to receive Communion. This litany was moved sometime before the tenth century, when adult catechumens were no longer common in Constantinople. At first, the litany was placed before the Trisagion ("Holy God, Holy and Mighty..."), because this was where the Liturgy in church began (the antiphons were processional psalms sung on the way to the church). When the procession was no longer common, the antiphons came to be sung in church, making a new beginning for the Liturgy. The litany of peace was moved accordingly to its present position before the first antiphon. The purpose of the Litany, then, was to give the faithful a chance to settle down and organize themselves for prayer. This is the meaning of the first petition, "In peace (that is, "in good order") let us pray to the Lord."

In this litany we pray for three different kinds of peace. The first, "In peace let us pray to the Lord," is for simple peace in the congregation — no loud talking, no distractions, no rustling about, pay attention to the service. In the second petition, "for peace from on high," we pray for the spiritual peace promised by Christ: "Peace I leave with you, my peace I give to you. Not as the world gives do I give to you" (John 14:27). This is a deep spiritual peace coming from an interior commitment to do the will of God, to serve Him freely in righteousness, and is a gift of God. This may not always be reflected in external peace, since to seek the Kingdom of God might arouse the hostility of "the world," of that aspect of human society that opposes divine love. The third petition, "for peace in the whole world," is for an outward peace among human nations and groups. In the end even this kind of peace is not obtainable by human efforts alone, and so we beg the Lord for it. Because we are totally dependent on God for all good gifts, our response is: "Lord, have mercy."

There are some differences in the new translation of the litany of peace. In the 1964 translation we prayed for "the priesthood" in the petition for Church authorities. Now we pray for "the presbyterate," which better corresponds to the Greek word used here, *presbyteros* ("elder"). The English word priest derives from *presbyteros*, but actually translates the Greek word *hiereus*. The older translation, "seasonable weather," was often the brunt of comments such as, "so you're praying for 'seasonable' weather — snow-storms in the winter and heat waves in the summer." It will become "favorable (Greek, *eukrasias*) weather." The petition was actually to avoid violent weather, as the Anaphora of St. Basil puts it, "Grant us a healthful and agreeable climate and gentle showers upon the earth that it may be fruitful." Travel by "air" has been added to meet a modern need. Finally, the stronger word, "commit," has been chosen to replace "commend" in the final petition, "Let us commit ourselves and one another, and our whole life, to Christ our God."

Prayers "of the Antiphons"

The prayer said by the priest to conclude the Litany summarizes the meaning of our petitions. Since "mercy" is mentioned over and over again, we pray to God, who is "merciful without limits" (Ephesians 2:4). We ask Him to "look with compassion on us" (Psalm 25:16), and to "show us the riches of your tender mercy." Much of the wording of the prayers said in the Liturgy comes from Sacred Scripture, and represents the Church's meditation on God's word. For this reason, it is appropriate that this prayer should be proclaimed publicly by the priest.

This prayer, called now the "prayer of the first antiphon," is very ancient and is one in a series of three prayers. The other two were moved to conclude the small litanies, generally no longer said, between the first and second and second and third antiphons. The third prayer, addressed to our Lord Jesus Christ, was actually the first prayer, said silently by the priest as the deacon proclaimed the litany: "Now hear the requests of your servants that will benefit them and give us the knowledge of your truth [Hebrews 10:26] in the present time, granting life eternal in the age to come." The second prayer was actually the prayer of blessing over the faithful, corresponding to the blessing of the catechumens. Its text is the same as the first part of the common ambon prayer said at the end of the Liturgy.

The Antiphons

After the opening litany of peace, we sing an office of three "antiphons," hymns of praise in celebration of God's love for us and all His creation. An antiphon is a psalm sung with a short refrain, for example, "Through the prayers of the Theotokos, O Savior, save us," or "O Son of God, risen from the dead, save us who sing to you, Alleluia!" The troparion which is sung at "Glory to the Father..." for the second antiphon is longer, the well-known and beloved Hymn of the Incarnation, "O only-begotten Son and Word of God...". The final refrain for the third antiphon is the troparion of the day. On feasts of our Lord, the troparion of the feast is the refrain for each verse of the antiphon. The antiphons are a changeable part of the Divine Liturgy. There is one set for Sundays, one set for weekdays, and unique sets for each of the feasts of our Lord. On certain occasions the Typica (Psalms 102, 145 and the Beatitudes) replace the antiphons. The Typica actually have their origin in a monastic rite for Holy Communion where there was no priest.

One of the most important hymns of the Liturgy is sung as a conclusion to the second antiphon, "O only begotten Son and Word of God...". This has become one of the favorite Byzantine hymns of all time. Emperor Justinian, who built the Great Church of Haghia Sophia, introduced it into the Liturgy, and, by tradition, was its author, though he may only have commissioned it. This hymn succinctly proclaims the very center of the Christian mystery. In Jesus, God became a human being, but remained God "without change." Since God is the creator and sustainer of the universe, it is impossible and inconceivable that He could ever not be God. Yet He has accepted the fullness of the human experience of life as a human being, even to the point of death on the cross. St. Paul expressed this mystery well in his Epistle to the Philippians 2:5-11. Being God, Jesus could not be conquered by death, and arose from the dead as a human being in the power of God. The resurrection of Jesus, however, was not for Himself alone, but brought the fullness of life into human existence. Therefore, we sing, "You were also crucified, O Christ, our God, and by death have trampled death."

The third antiphon concludes with a variable refrain, the troparion of the day or feast. The entrance hymn and the troparion and kontakion sung in the Divine Liturgy are actually part of the third antiphon, just as the Hymn of the Incarnation is part of the second antiphon. The troparion and kontakion are both taken from the daily offices (vespers and matins) and were meant as a variation on the refrain for the psalm. Therefore, they are like the keynote hymns for the particular mystery celebrated or holy person honored. In the Byzantine tradition, almost all of the Church's daily changing meditation on Scripture and the life of faith are contained in the offices of vespers and matins. Unfortunately, these offices are often ignored in parish practice. The Church has now directed the restoration of these offices, "Where [the] practice of celebrating the Divine Praises has diminished, if not completely disappeared, the ancient tradition should be restored without delay, so as not to deprive the faithful of a privileged source of prayer, nourished by treasures of authentic doctrine" (Congregation for the Eastern Churches Instruction, *Applying the Liturgical Prescriptions of the Code of Canons of the Eastern Churches*, 98).

We know from ancient manuscripts that the antiphons were originally sung as people processed from church to church. In first millennium Constantinople, there were no distinct parish churches as we know them today. There were many churches built to honor particular saints or as neighborhood devotional centers; however, these were not "parishes" as in our day. There was only one pastor, the bishop, and there was only one parish in the city. All the neighborhood churches were only extensions of the Great Church, Holy Wisdom (*Haghia Sophia*).

Frequently, one worship location was designated as "the church" for that day. If the main Liturgy was at, say, the church of Saints Sergius and Bacchus, then the people would meet at another church, say, the Church of the Mother of God at Blachernae, say a litany and prayer then process to St. Theodore's (since there was no public transportation then, cities were more compact and people could walk easily from one place to another). As they processed the people, led by cantors, would sing a psalm with a troparion (refrain). When they reached a church, they would stop briefly, the deacon would chant a litany and the priest would proclaim a prayer, and then they would process again to the next place, singing another psalm. These psalms were called "antiphons" because each verse of the scriptural psalm was alternated with a short hymn of the church called a "refrain" (in Greek, "troparion"). The last psalm with troparia that they sang would be Psalm 94, which we have already noted was a perfect entrance psalm, and has become our present-day third antiphon. The prayer that was said with the third antiphon was a prayer of entrance into the church: "Lord, our Master and God, who established orders and armies of angels and archangels for the service of your glory in heaven, make this our entrance an entrance of holy angels, concelebrating with us and glorifying your goodness." This prayer is still said today, at the little entrance.

In cities outside of Constantinople, and even there later in history when these processions became too much to maintain, the people simply gathered in church and sang the psalms one after another, with the litanies of the deacon and prayers of the priest in between.

When the antiphons became a part of the ordinary Liturgy, some changes crept in. First of all, it was no longer necessary to sing the whole psalm, so it was shortened to three or four verses. All the churches kept the practice of singing special antiphons on feast days of our Lord, with the troparion of the feast as the refrain for the third antiphon, but these, too, were reduced to three or four verses. The Greek and Melkite Churches introduced antiphons for feasts of the Mother of God. The Russian Church sings three verses of the antiphon but shortens the Typical Psalms (102 and 145), while singing all the Beatitudes.

Our Church books usually give three or four verses for each antiphon. However, it has become the standard practice in the Ruthenian Church in America in the last couple of generations to sing only the first verse and the doxology of the first and second antiphons.   Often the third antiphon was completely eliminated, which was a shame, since it is the most important of the three, an invitation to all to enter into worship of God in the Divine Liturgy: "Come, let us sing joyfully to the Lord; let us acclaim God our Savior" (Psalm 94:1).   Sometimes on feasts of our Lord the psalm verses of the third antiphon are compressed and the troparion is sung only once.   Sometimes this troparion, which to our mind is no longer a real refrain, is replaced completely by a shorter phrase from the second antiphon.

Because the office of the three antiphons originated in the city of Constantinople, it is a characteristic feature of the Byzantine tradition.   Other Eastern Churches, such as the Copts, the Syrians, the Maronites, the Armenians, the Chaldeans and others, do not begin the public part of the Liturgy with these antiphons; some did adopt the Hymn of the Incarnation.

Greek Churches very often eliminate the psalm verses altogether, but keep the refrains.   This illustrates a common liturgical tendency.   When the Liturgy is shortened, for whatever reason, it's usually the Scripture that is the first to go, even in the first millennium.   Thus the reading from the Old Testament was dropped; the prokeimenon was reduced to two verses of the psalm; the Communion hymn was reduced to one verse of the psalm; the antiphons were reduced to three (sometimes four) verses of the psalm; and the psalm verses between the stanzas of the Trisagion and the Cherubikon were dropped out.   I wish this were a practice that could be reversed.

We must ask a simple question: when the stational processions from church to church in Constantinople were dropped, why did the Church keep the office of the antiphons?   It would seem that their original purpose was no longer in place.   However, the antiphons now do serve another purpose, for they begin our Liturgy with hymns of praise and glorification of the God who is our Creator and Sanctifier.   At the same time, it is a part of the Liturgy most subject to "reform," that is, not in the sense of twisting out of shape, but of re-discovering basic principles.   Looking at the whole Liturgy from beginning to end, and being under the constraint of not making it too long, the authorities of the Church might decide to somewhat curtail this section so as to permit other important parts to be retained. The important goal is that we open our worship with the glorification of the God who is our Creator and Sanctifier. Whenever a modification is made in the Liturgy, not everyone will agree with it, for our prayer is too close to the center of our faith and to our relationship with God. What is more important, though, is that our Liturgy is the act of a community under the leadership of our bishops. We are not seeking our own will, but to acknowledge the presence of God together in the Body of Christ that is the Church.

Troparia and Kontakia

There are prayers and hymns that stay the same at every Divine Liturgy because at every Liturgy we remember and make present again the central mystery of our faith, that our Lord Jesus Christ died on the cross for us so that He might rise and give us the gift of everlasting life. Therefore, in every Liturgy of St. John Chrysostom, we quote John 3:16, "God loved the world so much that he gave his only Son, so that everyone who believes in him might not perish but might have eternal life." St. Paul tells us that, in the same way, we, too, "were buried with Christ Jesus through baptism into death [that is, death to sin, but at the end of our lives, also physical death], so that, just as Christ was raised from the dead by the glory of the Father, we too might live in newness of life" [that is, in a Christ-like life in this world, and eternal life with him in eternity]. Every time that we celebrate the Liturgy, we fulfill our Lord's command, "Whoever wishes to save his life will lose it, but whoever loses his life for my sake and that of the gospel will save it" (Mark 8:35). This is why we sing the same hymns and say the same prayers at every Liturgy, to signify this "Paschal Mystery" of our Lord's death and resurrection. As St. John Chrysostom said, "It is always Pascha" (Greek for the Hebrew *Pesach*, "Passover").

At the same time, there are also hymns that change at every Divine Liturgy. This is because the central Paschal Mystery reveals itself in many diverse ways in our life, and so we celebrate it in the mysteries of our Lord's life — His birth, baptism, transfiguration, resurrection — and in His many different words and deeds for which St. John tells us that there are not enough books in the whole world to record (see John 21:25). We also remember how the holy people of God have lived out this mystery in their lives, from the Virgin Mary, who submitted to God's plan in obedience and brought forth the salvation of the world, to the martyrs and confessors who suffered physically to witness to Christ, to the bishops and teachers who proclaimed the gospel both in word and deed. All of these are remembered by the changeable hymns and readings of the Church, which include the troparion, kontakion, prokeimenon, alleluia verses, Communion hymns and others.

The word "troparion" itself means refrain. As we have seen, the troparion was originally the refrain of the third antiphon. It is also sung at the end of vespers and at the beginning and end of matins. In a certain way, therefore, the troparion may be said to be the keynote hymn of the liturgical day, and each troparion reveals another aspect of the mystery of Christ's loving salvation.

After the doxology, the daily kontakion is sung. The word kontakion means "scroll" in Greek, and this might strike us as very strange. A kontakion was a lengthy hymn that was originally sung at matins between Psalm 50 and the Psalms of Praise (148-150). It usually had twenty-four variable stanzas (called *oikosi*), and what we today call the kontakion was the *proemion*, the "refrain that was written at the beginning." Because of its length, therefore, this liturgical hymn, or, better, series of hymns, was written on its own scroll, which the cantor unrolled when it was time to sing it. In matins today, only the kontakion itself (the "proemion") and the first oikos (often written "ikos" in the Slavonic tradition) are sung. I've gone through this long explanation so that we can understand why certain names are given to hymns and how they entered the Divine Liturgy from the daily offices of the Church. What is most important is that both the troparion and kontakion tell us about our relationship in faith and love to God, one in the Holy Trinity.

The troparion and kontakion are drawn from the texts of the daily offices, the cycle of daily services including Vespers (evening prayer), Matins (or better, "orthros," "the rising service"), and the little hours, which sanctify the day of faith. In the middle of the last century, there was a tendency to de-emphasize the importance of these offices in order to focus on the central mystery of the Divine Liturgy, in which we receive Communion in the holy body and blood of our Lord. The daily offices, however, are an extension of the Liturgy, and in them is contained the fullness of the Church's meditation on the death and resurrection of our Lord which is made present again in the Eucharist. "The Divine Praises continuously rekindle the spirit of vigilance in the desire for the return of the Lord and sanctify the whole day; recalling the memory of the presence of the Lord, they distribute his grace, permeating and inserting all of existence into the trinitarian life" (*Applying the Liturgical Prescriptions of the Code of Canons of the Eastern Churches*, 96). The troparion and kontakion are elements of our daily offices that have found their way into the Divine Liturgy, and become, in Pope John Paul II's words, the "continuation of the Word which is read, understood, assimilated and finally sung... sublime paraphrases of the biblical text, filtered and personalized through the individual's experience and that of the community" (*Orientale Lumen* 10).

The Trisagion

After the third antiphon, which concludes by the singing of the changeable troparion and kontakion, the priest exclaims, "For you are holy, our God, and we give glory to you, Father, Son and Holy Spirit, now and ever and forever." This doxology actually concludes a long prayer, called the prayer of the Trisagion (Greek for "thrice-holy"), which introduces the hymn of the same name. The Trisagion is certainly one of the favorite hymns in the history of the Byzantine Church, and it is sung in many places in the worship of the Church outside of the Divine Liturgy.

At one time, the Trisagion was an ancient hymn of entry even older than the antiphons. In the Trisagion's first appearance in history — at the Ecumenical Council of Chalcedon in the year 451 — it was sung as the bishops entered the church. In the present Liturgy, it is sung three times, then once more after a doxology. In the Greek usage, the deacon introduces this final singing by saying *dunamis*, which means, "with power," or "more loudly." Originally there were psalm versicles between the first three chantings, which probably were the verses sung today by the bishop at the beginning of a Hierarchial Liturgy: "Lord, Lord, look down and bless this vineyard which your right hand has planted...."

The Trisagion is one of the most important hymns in Eastern Christianity. There was, in fact, a controversy between the Oriental Churches (the Copts, Armenians and Syrians who did not accept the Council of Chalcedon) and the Orthodox Church about the meaning of this hymn. The Oriental Orthodox applied it entirely to Christ, and therefore made various insertions, for example, "Holy God, Holy and Mighty, Holy and Immortal, crucified for us, have mercy on us." The meaning, therefore, is that Jesus is God, all-powerful and eternal. The Byzantines, on the other hand, consistently applied it to the Holy Trinity: "Holy God [the Father], Holy and Mighty [the Son], Holy and Immortal [the Spirit]: have mercy on us." The Ecumenical Patriarch Germanos explained the Trisagion as our gift to God, "Like the Magi, we bring gifts to Christ — faith, hope and love like gold, frankincense, and myrrh — and like the bodiless hosts [angels] we cry in faith: 'Holy God,' that is the Father; 'Holy Mighty,' that is the Son and Word, for He has bound the mighty devil, made Him who had dominion over death powerless through the cross and has given us life by trampling on him; 'Holy Immortal,' that is, the Holy Spirit, the giver of life, through whom all creation is made alive and cries out 'Have mercy on us'" (*On the Divine Liturgy*, 25).

There is an explicit witness to how this hymn was composed in a fragment of a document found in the ancient library of the Patriarch Photius. This author said that it was a combination of the passage from the Prophecy of Isaiah, where the heavenly hymn of the angels, "Holy, holy, holy," was revealed (hence the name of the hymn, Trisagion, Thrice-holy) and Psalm 41:3, "Holy is God, strong and living" (changed to immortal for the sake of the chant). Interestingly, this is not the present Septuagint text of the psalm, but is found in an alternate version of Scripture. The hymn is unusual, in that the first phrase makes a statement and the second phrase asks for the blessing of mercy. Literally it reads: "Holy is God; He is holy and strong (or mighty); He is holy and immortal: (then addressed to God) have mercy on us."

As we have seen, the priest's prayer at the little entrance introduces us to the concept that the Liturgy we celebrate is a union of the worship of God in heaven by the angels and by us mortals here on earth. The prayer that the priest says before the singing of the Trisagion also addresses God whose heavenly throne is described by the prophet Isaiah (chapter 6) and surrounded by hosts of angels proclaiming His holiness, "Holy God, dwelling in your heavenly sanctuary, praised by the seraphim with the thrice-holy hymn, glorified by the cherubim, and adored by all the heavenly powers." Like Isaiah, then, we, still on earth, implore God to purify us that we may offer worthy praise to Him: "You have allowed us, your humble and unworthy servants, to stand at this very hour before the glory of your holy altar to offer you due worship and praise. Accept, O Master, from the lips of us sinners the thrice-holy hymn and visit us in your goodness. Forgive us every offense, voluntary and involuntary; sanctify us, soul and body, and grant that we may worship you in holiness all the days of our life."

Angels, in fact, have a key role in the Liturgy in which they have both a symbolic and real role. Our Liturgy on earth is a mystical representation of the heavenly angelic liturgy. The symbolism here points to something real: the Liturgy indeed unites us with glorification beyond our human limitations. If the Liturgy were just for this world, it would be a hopeless exercise; it could not possibly deliver what it promises. It would be an empty promise, and meaningless words and gestures. If the Liturgy were simply a heavenly, spiritual reality, with no relationship to our lives on earth and justice among peoples and nations, then it would also be meaningless, a flight from reality, a haven from the turmoil of the world. Angels are the connection with reality. They make real the abstract idea of the union of earthly and heavenly realities that gives the Liturgy its force to actually and truly change human life.

The presence of angels may also be a symbol of the presence of God. After the ascension of our Lord, the eternal reality is Jesus at the right hand of the Father interceding for us. Jesus alone is the eternal High Priest. Since, from Scripture, we see that the angels surround the throne of God constantly, proclaiming His holiness, if Christ is truly present among us now, then the angels are truly just as present. The further conclusion is, of course, that our worship is equal in dignity to the heavenly worship. Angels and mortals commingle, and we "represent the Cherubim."

The Readings from Scripture

While the Trisagion is being sung, the celebrant processes to the presbyteral chairs behind the holy table. After the hymn is completed, the Liturgy of the Word takes place. Our faith, our community, our Church, our Liturgy are all established on the text of the Scriptures, of the Bible. The Liturgy is full of Old Testament psalms and canticles as well as prayers that either quote the Scriptures directly or paraphrase them.

The Jewish synagogue service was built around the reading of Scripture and commentary or teaching on it. The Gospel of St. Luke tells of the presence of our Lord Jesus Christ at a Sabbath synagogue service in Nazareth. The Gospel tells us, "[Jesus] stood up to read and was handed a scroll of the prophet Isaiah. He unrolled the scroll and found the passage where it was written: [the text of Isaiah 61:1-2 is given]. Rolling up the scroll, he handed it back to the attendant and sat down, and the eyes of all in the synagogue looked intently at him. He said to them, 'Today this scripture passage is fulfilled in your hearing'" (Luke 4:16-21). Thus we see that our Lord Himself is the model for the reading of Scripture in the Church, and for commenting on it in the sermon.

Scripture reading was likewise to become an essential part of Christian worship. The Divine Liturgy is not complete until there is some reading from the Word of God revealed to us. Indeed, one might say that the whole of the Liturgy is the fulfillment of the Scriptural command, "Do this in memory of me."

Up to the Trisagion, everything in the Liturgy is called the "enarxis," which means simply "the beginning." After the Trisagion, the reading of Scriptures is called the "Liturgy of the Word." Certainly, there is no announcement made of when the Liturgy of the Word begins, nor is it even thought that it would be a separate service, divided from the rest. However, I do think that some kind of transition should be made so that the Liturgy is not just one long action with little variation.

The readings from Scripture are part of the original structure of the Divine Liturgy. It seems that until the seventh century, there were probably three readings: Old Testament, an Apostolic Reading (that is, from the Acts of the Apostles or one of the letters of the apostles recognized as canonical by the Church) and a Gospel. The psalm, called the prokeimenon, was also considered a reading, but it has been reduced to the refrain verse and the first verse of the psalm. This illustrates the tendency to reduce the reading of Scripture. The word *prokeimenon* itself means, in Greek, "placed before," referring to the one verse of the psalm that is chosen and "placed before" the other verses and repeated as a refrain after each of these verses.

In earlier centuries, there was a homily (sermon) after each of the readings. This preaching was originally done by the person who read the Scripture, though later it was restricted to the priest. In modern Greece, preaching is still done often by educated lay theologians, since many of the clergy only receive a rudimentary education. The homily is designed to explain the reading to the congregation. The minister of the Church, then, should have a special skill in applying the inspired words of God to the particular circumstances and culture of the people he serves. For the majority of his congregation, the homily is still the most important moment of evangelization (spreading the Gospel). Therefore, it should not be omitted except for only the most serious reasons. It is deadly for the faith when the homily is ignored, either because of the indifference of the listeners or the lack of skill of the preacher.

Except for feasts, the Byzantine Church follows the practice of a continuous reading of the Epistles and Gospels, beginning on Pascha. There are actually three courses, or cycles: for Sundays; Saturdays; and Weekdays (Monday to Friday). The Saturday cycle was once very important, but has fallen into much disuse. Even people who come to Liturgy daily often skip Saturday, which has become in popular culture a weekend workday. In addition, many priests who have a Saturday evening Liturgy for Sunday, do not serve on Saturday morning.

There are some who advocate a reform of the cycle of readings, expanding it to a two or three or even a four-year cycle. I personally think this may possibly be a good idea, if it were done thoughtfully, with respect for tradition, particularly for the Sundays that have an office connected with the gospels.

In all the Liturgy of the Word, there is only one prayer said by the priest, before the Gospel while the Alleluia is being sung. This is a private prayer of the priest that was never meant to be said publicly. The priest asks that he and all the people be filled with the light of the Gospel so that it be not only a matter of words, but might transform our lives. At the same time, the Gospel book is censed by the deacon, or priest. This should not be anticipated during the first reading, for all should be paying attention to the word of God. After all, the deacon frequently asks us to "be attentive" during this part of the Divine Liturgy.

The Liturgy of the Word tells us that the Scripture is, in the first place, the oral and proclaimed word of God. For the sake of convenience and for the preservation of its meaning, it has been put down into written text, but the Word of God was never meant to be "closed up" in a book, but to be read aloud to a community of people. It is good for us that we have the Bible and can consult it and read it by ourselves as individuals, but we never "hear" it until we listen to it read aloud in the assembly of the Church. For this reason, it is important that its translation into our contemporary speech should be both "always worthy of the noble realties it signifies, set apart from the everyday speech of the street and the marketplace," and at the same time "within the grasp of all, even children and the uneducated" (Pope Paul VI). While Pope Paul was referring to the Liturgy, this should also be true for Scripture, as much as possible, while retaining fidelity to divine revelation, because Scripture is liturgical by its nature.

Litanies after the Gospel

Following the readings and before the entry with the gifts is the original place where the litany prayers were said. Intercession for people and their needs is an ancient part of the Liturgy, along with praise and Scripture. The Liturgy of the Word then follows this movement: glorification of God, then hearing God's Word, then supplication for our needs. In this way we do not begin by begging God for His favor, but by glorifying the Creator of all things, who loves us beyond comprehension. St. Paul wrote, "neither height, nor depth, nor any other creature will be able to separate us from the love of God in Christ Jesus, our Lord" (Romans 8:39). Certainly God, who feeds the birds of the air and knows all our needs (see Matthew 6:26, 32), and who said, "Ask and it will be given to you," (Matthew 7:7) will hear the prayer we offer in the Divine Liturgy and will respond appropriately.

The Liturgy now includes the following prayers at this point: the litany of fervent supplication, the litany for the catechumens and two prayers for the faithful. The litany of fervent supplication came into the Liturgy from offices that were said in times of special need. Therefore the insistence, over and over again, on imploring the mercy of God. In Church Slavonic it is called the *Suhubaja Ektenije* (the "Redoubled Litany,") because the "Lord, have mercy" is redoubled and sung three times. This litany is not a replacement for the litany of peace, which was a prayer for the faithful, said after the dismissal of the catechumens. It was introduced into the Liturgy when catechumens were no longer actually dismissed, because the original concept was that before baptism, catechumens could not actually pray, because "their prayer was not yet pure." (a formula found in various Fathers). Their faith was not yet perfect.

The litany for the catechumens is not a prayer by the catechumens, but for the catechumens by the faithful. When it came about that there were very few adult converts, no one actually left the church at this point of the Liturgy although the dismissal continued to be said. The dismissal for the (mostly) non-existent catechumens then caused some problems for liturgical commentators. For example, Nicholas Gogol in the nineteenth century said that when the litany is said, we must consider ourselves as catechumens who have not yet been completely evangelized.

Our Church has not said this litany for many years, but would do so if catechumens, those preparing for baptism, were actually present, though they will not be dismissed from the church. It would be wonderful if our church actually started evangelizing again and that we would have many catechumens. Interestingly, to this day, the priest does not open the antimension on the holy table until after the point of the dismissal of catechumens, because the mystery of the Eucharist as the death (which is depicted on it) and the resurrection of Christ was not yet revealed to them.

Once the catechumens were dismissed, the faithful could pray for the needs of the world. This is why the litany of peace, which is now said at the beginning of the Liturgy, was originally said here. The Russian Church still says four petitions from this litany at this point if a deacon is serving.

After this, the priest says two prayers of the faithful in a quiet voice. The Liturgy turns from supplication to preparation for the great mystery that is to follow. In the first of these prayers, the priest, who is about to ask the Father to send the Holy Spirit, "upon us and upon the gifts brought forth," asks God to "enable us, whom you have placed in this your ministry through the power of your Holy Spirit, to call upon you at all times and in all places without condemnation or blame." This is even more explicit in the corresponding prayer from the Liturgy of St. Basil: "Through the power of your Holy Spirit, enable us for this service so that, standing without condemnation before your holy glory, we may offer you a sacrifice of praise; for you alone empower all we do." No one can offer the Liturgy or even pray by his own power, but only in the grace of the Holy Spirit. Therefore, we must ask God over and over again for a purity of conscience.

Originally there were three prayers of the faithful: one was said quietly while the deacon chanted the litany, the second was said publicly when the litany was concluded, and the third was a prayer of dismissal during the bowing of heads. The third prayer is no longer there, and some think it may be the prayer now said at the bowing of heads after the Our Father. At one time, those faithful not going to Communion were dismissed from the church before the anaphora along with the catechumens and penitents. The thought was that, if you stayed, you went to Communion, since it is not simply our individual share in the body and blood of Christ, but our solidarity with the whole people of God, who make up the body of Christ that is the Church (Ephesians 1:22-23). To have refused Communion, then, was like coming to a meal and not eating.

For Your Reflection

1. How do you believe the Divine Liturgy connects us to the Kingdom of God?

2. How do the Scripture readings prepare us to celebrate the Eucharist?

3. Are there many catechumens in your parish? Why do you think this is so?

Chapter Three — The Oblation

The next section of the Liturgy, the Eucharistic oblation, begins with the bringing of the gifts of bread and wine to the holy table for the prayer of offering. As such, it is a fulfillment of the Gospel command, when Jesus "took" bread, blessed it, broke it and gave it to his disciples." The great entrance is the "taking" of the bread, even though not every ceremony connected with it is from apostolic times.

In its origin, this rite was truly a "great" entrance. At least in the Church of Haghia Sophia in Constantinople, the gifts were brought in from an outside building. They were then taken in procession through the center of the church. At first, the deacons alone brought the gifts into the church, where the celebrating bishop or priest met them before the altar and placed them on the holy table. To this very day, the bishop maintains this custom at Hierarchal Liturgies, waiting at the royal doors to receive the chalice and diskos from the priests and deacons.

The Cherubikon

The gifts of bread and wine are brought to the altar while the Cherubic Hymn is being sung. This hymn was written for the congregation so that they may participate in the procession of the gifts to the holy table. We can date the introduction of this hymn into the Liturgy to the time of the Emperor Justin II, in the year 573-574. The then Patriarch Euthyches complained about the chanting of Psalm 23:7-10 during the entrance of the gifts, because the refrain of this psalm is "Let him enter, the king of glory." For the patriarch this was a theological error; the gifts of bread and wine were not yet the body and blood of Christ, and the "King of glory" is not entering. Euthyches said, "They act stupidly, who have taught the people to sing this psalm... the people say that they bear in the King of glory and refer in this way to the things being brought up, even though they have not yet been consecrated by the high-priestly invocation [i.e. the anaphora]." Of course, some will note that the Cherubikon makes a similar point, "That we may receive the King of all," and that the faithful continue to honor the gifts that are being brought forth.

The over-all theme of the Cherubikon is one common to the Byzantine Liturgy: our earthly Liturgy is offered in union with the heavenly worship of the angelic choirs. We see this also in the prayer of the entrance and in the hymn of victory ("Holy, holy, holy...") at the anaphora itself. In the Liturgy there is a constant stream of interest in angels and their relationship with us "mortals." The hymn itself mentions the Trisagion ("Thrice-holy"), sung by the angels and its relationship to the Trinity. Thus, it brings us into the presence of the Trinity. Therefore, we must "set aside all earthly cares."

Some have interpreted this to mean that our Liturgy is totally mystical, that it is concerned with spiritual and heavenly matters, and that, therefore, the Byzantine Church is not concerned with works of charity and the mundane needs of the people. However, this has not been borne out in history, for the Church in the Byzantine Empire was quite concerned about issues of social welfare. The hymn itself uses the words of the parable of the sower in the Gospel of Luke (Luke 8:4-15). The "earthly cares" (in Greek, *biotikin merimnan*) are the "anxieties and riches and pleasures of life" (this is the translation of the New American Bible, the Greek for "anxieties of life," uses the same words as the liturgical translation, "earthly cares") that fail to produce mature fruit. The hymn does not tell us to ignore charity to the needy, but warns us against a love of riches and pleasures that would choke off the life of the spirit, a message that we can truly heed in our country today. The Cherubikon is also variable, as there are proper cherubic hymns for the Liturgy of the Presanctified Gifts, for Great Thursday and for Great Saturday.

Our translation of the Cherubikon now reads: "Let us who mystically represent the cherubim and sing the thrice-holy hymn to the life-creating Trinity, now set aside all earthly cares, that we may receive the King of all, invisibly escorted by angelic hosts. Alleluia! Alleluia! Alleluia!" There is only one change from the translation we've become accustomed to: in the second part of the Cherubikon, "welcome" becomes "receive." The word here literally means more than welcome, but to actually "receive," as "to receive in Communion." The Cherubikon, then, looks forward to the ultimate goal of the Divine Liturgy, that we are united to God in the reception of Holy Communion. Perhaps it was this word that justified the hymn — we are not simply venerating bread and wine that are being brought in, but we are looking towards the reception of these gifts in Holy Communion, when we will be united with God in the Holy Trinity.

The Prayer of the Cherubikon

During the chanting of the Cherubic Hymn, the priest quietly says the prayer of the Cherubic Hymn, with hands raised as a sign of openness to God. As he does this, the deacon censes the holy table on all sides as well as the gifts on the altar of preparation. The incensation of the people was added later.

The prayer of the Cherubikon is clearly very different from previous prayers of preparation, the two prayers of the faithful. It is much longer, it is addressed to Christ, and it is the only place in the Liturgy where the priest prays in the first person singular. It was the most recent prayer introduced into the Liturgy, in about the tenth century, as can be seen from documents. It serves as a private preparation of the priest before he proclaims the anaphora, again expressing the unworthiness of the priest to serve a Liturgy that is "divine," or "godly." Most people find this prayer to be quite beautiful.

The doxology of the prayer, in which Christ is called both "the One who offers and is offered, who receives and distributes" reflects the idea that it is Christ acting in the Liturgy, that He is giving Communion. This concept, which is quite important in

Byzantine theology and iconography, gave rise to a theological dispute in the year 1156, when a deacon, Soterichos Panteugenes, objected to this formulation. The synod of 1156 declared that Christ is both able to offer and receive because He is both God and man. With this prayer we are now ready to bring the gifts of bread and wine to the Holy Table.

The Great Entrance

After the priest concludes this prayer, the great entrance is made. Both the priests and deacons say the Cherubic Hymn privately three times, since because of their actions at this time, they cannot sing with the people. The priests, deacons and other servers go to the table of preparation where the gifts have been arranged. On the way the priest says, "O God, be merciful to me, a sinner." There are, in fact, many points in the Liturgy where the priest proclaims his unworthiness, because, as St. John Chrysostom said many times, the celebration of the Liturgy is beyond human, indeed, even angelic powers. What is impossible to men, though, is possible to God. The priest prays and acts only in the power of the Holy Spirit.

At the table of preparation, the priest censes the gifts. Then the deacon says, "Lift up, Reverend Father," and the priest replies, "Lift up your hands to the holy gifts and bless the Lord." This is a quotation from Psalm 133 (Hebrew 134): 2, but the Greek itself is indeterminate, saying literally, "lift up your hands to the holies." It is most often interpreted as "holy place," but this shows the difficulty of translation, for we are dealing here with something that was ambiguous in the original. The Commission chose "holy gifts," since the priest says this as he reaches out to take the gifts to the holy table, but this is an interpretation.

The priest gives the deacon the diskos and aer, which is the large veil that covers the gifts. The celebrant takes the chalice and the concelebrants other holy objects, such as the spoon and the lance. As the entrance is made, certain commemorations are said aloud. At one point in history, as the priest went through the center of the church, the people asked him to pray for their intentions.

Later, this was formalized into a particular series of commemorations for the church and civil authorities in order to bring order to the process. When this happened, the commemorations began to be said aloud and the Cherubic Hymn was divided into two parts by these commemorations.

This was the most recent place in the Liturgy that commemorations for particular people were added; the first place was the anaphora (the diptychs), the second the litanies, then the great entrance. The recitation of the commemorations aloud now interrupts the Cherubikon at the Divine Liturgy, but not at the Presanctified Liturgy, which keeps the original custom of no loud commemorations. I think, in fact, that the great entrance of the Presanctified Liturgy is the one place in the Byzantine Liturgy were there is a built-in period of silence. The Cherubic Hymn for the Presanctified Liturgy differs from that at the Divine Liturgies of St. John Chrysostom and St. Basil, because the gifts have already been consecrated, and so we sing: "Now the powers of heaven are serving with us invisibly, for behold the King of glory enters. They escort the mystical sacrifice already accomplished. Let us draw near with faith and love, that we may become partakers of life everlasting. Alleluia! Alleluia! Alleluia!" The same themes are present, though, for we are serving together with the angels and we are invited to receive our Lord in Communion.

When he reaches the holy table, the priest places the chalice there and takes the diskos from the deacon. He removes the small veils, censes the aer and replaces it over the gifts. As he does this, he says the troparion of Good Friday, "The noble Joseph took down your most pure body from the cross. He wrapped it in a clean shroud and with fragrant spices laid it in burial in a new tomb."

For some ancient liturgical commentators, each moment of the Liturgy was interpreted to correspond to a moment in our Lord's life. These interpretations were meant to be an aid to piety, but they must be understood correctly. The Liturgy is not simply a remembrance of what happened in history, but it is the presence of God in our lives now, as well as a proclamation of the future coming of our Lord. The Liturgy, then, looks to both the past and the future. Most of the historical interpretations are not explicitly mentioned in the Liturgy, but the troparion at this point affirms one of the most ancient allegories: the great entrance as the burial procession of our Lord. This interpretation is already found in Theodore of Mopsuestia at the end of the fourth century, and so the Good Friday troparion recalling the burial of Jesus is said.

When the gifts have been covered again by the aer, the priest censes the gifts as he says the end of Psalm 50, "In your goodness show favor to Zion, rebuild the walls of Jerusalem." The deacon had said Psalm 50 while incensing the church. The very last words reveal the meaning of this psalm for the Liturgy, "then you will be offered young bulls on your altar." The Christian altar fulfills the sacrifices of the Old Law. There are no longer animal sacrifices, but the offering is now bread and wine, which are to become the body and blood of Christ.

The Dialogue with the Deacon

There follows a dialogue between the priest and the deacon. This was originally said between the celebrant and his con-celebrants. The celebrant first asks for a remembrance in prayer, and the con-celebrants answered, "May the Lord God remember your priesthood in His Kingdom." Then the celebrant said, "Pray for me, my con-celebrants," and they replied in the words of the angel Gabriel to Mary, "The Holy Spirit shall come upon you, and the power of the Most High shall overshadow you" (Luke 1:35). The celebrant answers with an ancient formula found in the Liturgy, and adapted from Romans 8:26, "May the Spirit Himself concelebrate with us all the days of our lives." There is a parallel dialogue in the Roman rite, when the priest asks after the gifts are brought forward, "Pray, brothers and sisters, that my sacrifice and yours be acceptable..."

For many centuries the nature of this dialogue has been forgotten, and was relegated to the priest and deacon. However, the meaning indicates that this is a dialogue between concelebrants. It has been restored as such in the *Archieraticon* (the Bishop's Liturgicon) of 1973.

We see here repeated again the theology of the Liturgy that God is acting in and through our words and actions. Our offering of bread and wine becomes the Body and Blood of Christ, making us holy through deification, by the power of the Holy Spirit. Just as the angel announced to Mary that she would become the Mother of God, so too the gifts that enter accompanied by the invisible ranks of angels, bring us into union with God.

The Prayer of Approach to the Holy Table

After this dialogue, the priest says a prayer that is entitled in the liturgikon, the "prayer of offering" (in Greek, "of *proskomedia*"), a title that may be a little misleading. In the Roman Mass, when the gifts have been brought to the altar, the priest lifts up the bread and chalice separately and says a prayer of offering for each before the eucharistic prayer begins. This rite is called the offertory, and in Scholastic theology was considered essential for the Liturgy.

Because we live in the Western world, some theologians have tried to find something equivalent in the Byzantine Liturgy, but there simply is no parallel action. The formula, "prayer of offering," probably refers to all the prayers of the Liturgy following the great entrance, including the anaphora, which might be translated literally, "the offering," and refers to the prayer in which the bread and wine become the body and blood of Christ. The prayer, said immediately after the entrance of the gifts, might be called better, "The prayer of approach to the holy table." Here is the text of the prayer:

> "Lord God Almighty, who alone are holy and receive the sacrifice of praise from those who call upon you with their whole heart, accept also the prayer of us sinners; bring us to your holy altar; enable us to offer you gifts and spiritual sacrifices for our sins and for the people's failings. Make us worthy to find favor in your sight that our sacrifice may be pleasing to you, and that the good Spirit of your grace may rest on us, on these gifts here present, and on all your people."

We see, then, that the priest prays for himself and those celebrating with him that they might be accepted at God's altar. Despite this, it is not a private prayer of the priest, because the "spiritual sacrifice" that he is about to offer is not only for himself, but for all the people. The purpose, therefore, is that all present, priests, deacons and people might "find favor in your sight that our sacrifice may be pleasing to you, and that the good Spirit of your grace may rest on us, on these gifts here present, and on all your people." To this petition and its doxology, the people respond "Amen."

This prayer seems to be one of the key texts of the Divine Liturgy. Three prayers give the basic structure to our offering: this prayer, which prepares us for the anaphora; the anaphora itself; and the prayer of thanksgiving after Communion. Here the priest addresses God as "the only One who is holy." "Holy" means completely other, blessed and sanctified and good, as opposed to our unworthiness. This reality is addressed frequently in the Liturgy. Before receiving Communion, we chant solemnly, "One is holy, one is Lord, Jesus Christ, to the glory of God the Father." In his private prayer before the great entrance, the priest also proclaims his unworthiness to offer the spiritual sacrifice: "No one who is bound by carnal desires and pleasures is worthy to come to you, to approach you, or to minister to you, the King of Glory; for to minister to you is great and awesome even to the heavenly powers themselves."

The priest is unworthy in two ways, in the first place because he is human and is doing something that belongs to God. John Chrysostom tells us, "The priest does nothing, nor is the right accomplishment of the offered gifts due to human nature; but the grace of the Spirit being present, and coming down on every altar makes complete that mystical sacrifice; for even though a man be present, it is God who works through him" (Homily 50 on Pentecost). In the second place, the priest is also unworthy because of his personal sins. Therefore, in the prayer he asks God to "enable us to offer you gifts and spiritual sacrifices for our sins and for the people's failings." Though this prayer is said by and for the priest celebrating the Liturgy, and the "we" that is spoken is for himself and for his con-celebrants, we see here that the people, who say "Amen" to this prayer, are also associated in the sacrifice and beg forgiveness through the words uttered by the priest. The only difference is that the priest acknowledges that he is a conscious sinner, who should know better, while the people sin out of ignorance, and their transgressions are "failings," acts done out of ignorance. This is not meant to be patronizing nor condescending to the people, only the sincere confession that we can say only that we are sinners, but are unable to judge others. The sacrifice is clearly offered by all the people present, and all receive the gift of the Spirit in return.

The prayer states that the sacrifice we offer is a "spiritual sacrifice." In divine Providence, there is, of course, only one perfect sacrifice, offered once and for all by Jesus with his own blood upon the cross. Because He is God, this sacrifice is eternal, and is present everywhere and at all times. The Divine Liturgy that we offer is essentially the presence of this one sacrifice, by which God loved the world. At the same time, the bloody sacrifice of the cross can be located in human history to a particular place and a particular time. It is eternally manifested through the resurrection, by which Christ was glorified for the salvation and deification of all human beings. The Liturgy insists that the sacrifice we offer in ritual is a "spiritual sacrifice," an "unbloody sacrifice," a "sacrifice of praise," in which the one true sacrifice in present spiritually and mystically. We are truly saved by the cross and the resurrection, but we do not have to suffer the cross historically and physically. Our "sacrifice of praise" must come from hearts willing to keep God's commandments and to worship Him in truth.

This is impossible to our mere human powers. This is why we end the prayer by asking, "that the good Spirit of Your grace rest on us, on these gifts here present, and on all your people." That the Divine Liturgy happens only in the grace of the Spirit, is a common theme of the Liturgy. This looks forward within the Liturgy to the sanctification of the gifts by the Holy Spirit, who makes the bread and wine to be the body and blood of our Lord, and to our communion in these gifts in "the fullness of the Spirit," as we sing, "we have seen the true Light, we have received the heavenly Spirit." This prayer, then, asks that God bring us to the place in our life where we will find forgiveness and life and union with Him.

The Prayer of Approach in the Liturgy of St. Basil

As we have seen, the prayers in the Liturgy of St. Basil are generally longer than the corresponding prayers in the Liturgy of St. John Chrysostom because they proclaim by specific examples from Scriptures the whole of the story of our salvation, our passage from darkness to light, from sin to righteousness, from death to life. This is very true of the Prayer of Approach in St. Basil's Liturgy, which places our oblation in the context of the sacrifices of the former covenants that were fulfilled by our Lord through His death on the cross and His life-giving resurrection. The priest prays, "Look upon us, O God, and behold this our spiritual worship, and accept it as you accepted the gifts of Abel, the sacrifices of Noah, the first-fruits of Abraham, the priesthood of Moses and Aaron, and the peace-offerings of Samuel."

In each of these instances, we see that God accepted a sacrifice that was offered with a sincere heart, and rejected false and hypocritical sacrifices. The story of Cain and Abel is well known. Here, "Cain brought an offering to the Lord from the fruit of the soil, while Abel... brought one of the best firstlings of his flock. The Lord looked with favor on Abel and his offering, but on Cain and his offering he did not" (Genesis 4:3-4). The wickedness in Cain's heart rose up in violence as he killed his brother out of jealousy. Noah's sacrifice was accepted because he alone on the face of the earth was righteous, while the rest of the human race was destroyed. Abraham became the father of the chosen people, rejecting Ur of the Chaldeans to go to the land promised him by God. Moses and Aaron codified the rites of this chosen people when God freed them from slavery in Egypt and Moses talked to God as a friend. In all these stories, we see God choosing those who offered pure sacrifices that nevertheless were only a foreshadowing of the true worship to come.

The prophet Samuel, son of Hannah was likewise chosen by God over Hophni and Phineas, the sons of the priest Eli. God said, "I will choose a faithful priest who shall do what I have in heart and mind" (1 Samuel 2:35). Samuel was to anoint Saul as king of Israel, and then reject him and later anoint David. Samuel foretold the true spiritual nature of the sacrifices of the New Covenant made by Jesus: "Does the Lord so delight in holocausts and sacrifices as in obedience to the command of the Lord? Obedience is better than sacrifice, and submission than the fat of rams" (1 Samuel 15:22). On the cross Christ offered His obedience to the Father in the perfect sacrifice that destroyed sin and death and brought resurrection. This sacrifice is identified with the Divine Liturgy, so that every time we serve the Liturgy, we offer the same "true worship from the hands of the apostles."

The prayer of approach to the holy table in the Liturgy of St. Basil, then, goes into greater detail about the nature of the worship we are offering to God. In the prayer, therefore, we address God by saying, "You created us and brought us into this life. You have shown us ways to salvation and have bestowed on us the revelation of heavenly mysteries." The priesthood of Christ thus fulfills all the promises of the first covenant. The priest prays, "O Lord, be pleased to make us servants of your new covenant and ministers of your holy mysteries." The priest offers this service in the name of all the people, so that it is the Liturgy of the whole Church.

This prayer expresses all the themes that we saw in the parallel prayer from the Liturgy of St. John Chrysostom. The priest, as a human being, is unable to offer a divine sacrifice except through the Holy Spirit. The prayer, therefore, affirms simply, "You yourself have appointed us to this service by the power of the Holy Spirit." This refers to the grace of the laying on of hands in ordination, by which the priest is able to proclaim the true worship of the community. As human nature is incapable of this, we must implore God to "receive us as we draw near Your holy altar so that we may be worthy to offer You this spiritual and unbloody sacrifice for our sins and for the people's failings." Here, as in the Liturgy of St. John Chrysostom, the priest acknowledges that he is a conscious sinner, who should know better, while the people sin out of ignorance. This prayer, in fact, also repeats an intercession, in almost the same words, that is found in the rites of ordination of a deacon, a priest and a bishop, that their ministry be acceptable even before the judgment seat of God. "May we who have been made worthy to minister without blame at your holy altar obtain the reward of faithful and wise stewards on the fearsome day of your just retribution." The human priest fulfills this function only in God's Spirit, when he leads all the faithful to the holy table of God's banquet.

The Kiss of Peace

Just as every anaphora is the fulfillment of Jesus' command to "do this in memory of me," so also our preparation to celebrate it fulfills another commandment. After the Prayer of Approach, the deacon exclaims, "Let us love one another, that with one mind we may profess." This sets before us another command of Christ recorded in the Gospel of St. Matthew: "If you bring your gift to the altar, and there recall that your brother has anything against you, leave your gift there at the altar, go first and be reconciled with your brother, and then come and offer your gift" (Matthew 5:23-24).

At one time, this was the signal for each person to turn to his neighbor in the church, and kiss them on the shoulder as a sign of reconciliation and love. This ritual kiss of peace was an external manifestation of a genuine inner spirit that we are willing to make peace with all our brothers and sisters in faith. The love intended here is a human reflection of divine love, which seeks always the good and the fullness of life in others, even to the point of giving our life for others, as Christ did on the cross. St. John explains in his first Letter, "Beloved, if God so loved us, we also must love one another. No one has ever seen God. Yet, if we love one another, God remains in us, and his love is brought to perfection in us" (1

John 4:11:12). It is unfortunate that our contemporary society constricts love to only physical affection.

The kiss of peace may be as ancient as the Gospel itself. In the Gospel of St. Luke, Jesus reproaches the Pharisee Simon when a woman washes Christ's feet and kisses them, "You did not give me a kiss, but she has not ceased kissing my feet since the time I entered" (Luke 7:45). That this was done at the Divine Liturgy in the first century is seen in the *Didache*, "Everyone that has a dispute with his companion shall not come together with you to break bread and give thanks until they be reconciled, that your sacrifice not be defiled" (14,2).

As is often the case, St. John Chrysostom is most eloquent on the meaning of the kiss of peace, "When we are about to participate in the sacred table, we are also instructed to offer a holy greeting.... we join souls with one another on that occasion by means of the kiss, so that our gathering becomes like the gathering of the apostles when, because all believed, there was one heart and one soul.... When the gift is set before us, let us, therefore, first become reconciled with one another and then proceed to the sacrifice" (The Eleventh Baptismal Instruction, 32-33). To prepare ourselves for the Eucharistic mystery, we must reconcile ourselves to one another, lest we be unworthy of His love by our hatred for another.

At one time, the following prayer, which has disappeared from present practice, accompanied the kiss of peace: "Lord Jesus Christ, Maker of love and Bestower of benefits, grant that we Your servants may love one another, as You have loved us, that we may approach You in faith and love in unity of mind and body and soul, and give praise to You and become partakers in Your holy mysteries and become worthy of your heavenly kingdom."

The evidence of the importance of this ritual is clear, but it is, in fact, no longer practiced in most Byzantine Churches. Only the priests and deacons still exchange the kiss of peace with one another, while the rite has fallen into disuse among the faithful, perhaps because of a fear of physical contact. However, much of this is simply cultural, and in some areas of the world people kiss one another much more freely. Thus the kiss of peace has always been exchanged in the Syriac Churches.

In Europe and America we are influenced by Western culture, which has stronger physical boundaries. We show affection within the family, but much more reluctantly to outsiders. Nonetheless, the deacon says, "let us love one another," and Christian love within the community is one of the foundations of a strong Church. For this reason the Roman Church, has reintroduced a sign of peace, albeit often a simple handshake. Many people see this as an important part of the Liturgy, but others are hesitant about it. Our Byzantine Church, for whatever reason, has been more reluctant to consider the restoration of this practice among the lay faithful. In an individualistic age, our personal relationship with God might be viewed as more significant than how we get along with one another. Whatever is the practice, it must be hoped that the Liturgy will bring genuine reconciliation among people, as St. John warned, ""If anyone says, 'I love God,' but hates his brother, he is a liar... whoever does not love a brother whom he has seen cannot love God whom he has not seen" (1 John 4:20).

The Profession of Faith

The deacon invites the faithful to exchange the kiss of peace by saying, "Let us love one another so that with one mind we may profess." The people respond, "The Father, and the Son and the Holy Spirit, the Trinity one in essence and undivided." We then confess our faith to one another.

Unity as charity, as strong bonds of Christian love in the community, is primary. We see that the usual way of looking at the church is here reversed. Today there is a tendency to dismiss doctrines as divisive. People tire of arguments about what is true. Many claim that, "it doesn't matter what you believe just so long as you have some kind of faith." Then, in reaction to this minimalist opinion, many others emphasize the importance of correct teaching, saying that you need to have the right faith before there can be community.

At this moment in the Liturgy we see that true profession of faith springs from a strong and loving community. At the same time, we also see a balance, in that a vague feeling of believing in "something" cannot replace true faith in the Holy Trinity. To truly love one another is to be not only of one heart, but also of one mind. There cannot be a focused love without a clear belief in the true God, for otherwise the community would splinter in a confusion of individual opinions. The purpose of the profession of faith is to build a strong community that can worship the true God in one mind and with one heart. Both are necessary and important. Without the "one mind," you have division and confusion, but without the "one heart" you have hatred and strife. Thus, in the Western Middle Ages, people were burnt at the stake for heresy.

There is a double response of the community to the deacon's invitation "to profess with one mind." The second is the creed itself, which we shall turn to later in this article. The first is the sung response which proclaims the most important aspect of our faith — that God is three persons, the Father, the Son, who has become incarnate for us in Jesus Christ our Lord, and the Holy Spirit, God giving himself to us and guiding us to all truth (John 16:13), and that there is only one God, "one in essence ("substance" in the earlier translation) and undivided."

This response to the deacon's invitation to the kiss of peace is the Liturgy's original summation of our faith. In the seventh century it was felt necessary to recite the creed in every Liturgy to strengthen our faith before the anaphora. Part of the Liturgy ever since, the creed explains in greater detail our simpler sung profession of faith. It prepares us to say the anaphora "with one heart and one mind," and to be united in the Communion of the body and blood of the one Lord, Jesus Christ.

This particular creed was chosen because it was the standard of belief of the first two ecumenical councils — that is, councils of the whole Church — that met in Nicaea (325) and Constantinople (381). In the fourth century, for an accurate expression of faith, it became necessary for the Church to declare and define more clearly its faith in the Holy Trinity. This creed was the basis for further definitions and expressions of faith, always under the guidance of the Holy Spirit.

The Creed itself is a threefold proclamation. The first part, "I believe," which expresses our faith in one God in Holy Trinity, is the longest and we will return to it. The second part beginning, "I profess," contains one proposition: "I profess one baptism for the remission of sins." This is an affirmation of the importance of our liturgical worship of God. Baptism here must be understood in a greater context. It includes our whole sacramental life of faith, of coming to enlightenment, of living the Gospel, of being sealed with the Holy Spirit, of communicating in the body and blood of our Lord, in repentance for the forgiveness of sins, of bringing about new life in marriage, of serving the people of God in ministry, of professing the power of God even in the human weakness of sickness and death. "Baptism" here stands for more than a single rite, but the reality of God acting in our lives, conforming us to his life and forming us into a worshiping community.

The third part of the Creed is an expression of our hope in God, "I expect the resurrection of the dead and the life of the world to come." Our confidence is in God even in the face of the greatest human tragedy, death. In our worship we shout out, "Christ is risen from the dead," believing with St. Paul, "Since death came through a human being, the resurrection of the dead came also through a human being. For just as in Adam all die, so too in Christ we shall be brought to life" (1 Corinthians 15:21-22).

The first part of the creed makes up the greater part of the text. Here we profess faith, which is more than just an opinion that there might be a God, but a total commitment of our minds and hearts to the truth as it has been revealed by God through Jesus Christ, the Son and Word of God.

Our faith is in one God in Holy Trinity: Father, Son and Holy Spirit, "one in essence and undivided." The word for "one in essence" in Greek is *homoousion*, which the Council of Nicaea used to describe Christ, proclaiming that He is truly God, one with the Father and not divided from Him. Likewise, when we say that God is "undivided," we mean that He is profoundly one in a way that is beyond our understanding. God is the one reality, the Source of all unity, one in essence and the Creator of all that is. As such, though the Trinity is clearly three persons, God always relates to us as one Divinity, who is Father, Son and Spirit.

Whenever God acts in our lives, He acts in Trinity, for God is one. We move and exist and have our being in God, our Creator and Father. As the Liturgy of St. Basil says, God the Father has revealed Himself "...in Jesus Christ, our Savior, who is our hope, the image of his goodness, the seal bearing his likeness," and as our Lord was to tell Philip, "Whoever has seen me has seen the Father" (John 14:9). Likewise the Letter to the Hebrews says, "In these last days, [God] spoke to us through a son, whom he made heir of all things and through whom he created the universe, who is the refulgence of his glory, the very imprint of his being" (Hebrews 1:2-3).

The work of salvation of Jesus Christ is described in the creed in detail, because though "one in essence with the Father... for us and for our salvation, he came down from heaven and was incarnate from the Holy Spirit and the Virgin Mary and became man." The creed echoes what St. Paul wrote, "that Christ died for our sins in accordance with the scriptures, that he was buried, that he was raised on the third day in accordance with the scriptures" (1 Corinthians 15:3-4). Again, the Liturgy of St. Basil tells us that "through him [the Son] the Holy Spirit has been revealed," who is "Life-creating Power, and the wellspring of sanctification." The "belief" part of the creed ends with the Church, not because it is a construction of human power, but because it is the divine gift of the Holy Spirit. By the recitation of the creed, therefore, every Liturgy becomes our proclamation of faith in God creating, redeeming and sanctifying us through the mystery of salvation which we are about to represent in our prayer of offering, the anaphora.

The creed was written originally in Greek. For us, and for many others in various times and places, it has been necessary to translate it into the vernacular language, or, at least, the language used in the Liturgy. Accurate translation is of particular importance in a creed, which uses technical terms with exactitude.

Unfortunately, words themselves do not have the same range of meanings from one language to another. This does not mean that the translation is wrong, or that it misrepresents our faith, but simply that we must be aware that all human language is a picture — an icon, if you will — of the reality that it reflects. For example, in Greek, the statement of our faith is that God is one *ousia* ("nature" in English) in three *hypostases* ("persons" in English). "Hypostasis" has a greater range of meaning than "person" in English, though this is the most accurate translation possible. Another set of words that has a different range of meanings is *anthropos* (a human being) and *aner* (a male, from which we get the name "Andrew," "manly"). We may have heard the saying, "The Greeks had a word for it." Here their words are more clear than the English "man," which, in different contexts, can mean both "a mortal being of the human nature," and a "male human being." Therefore, the original creed in Greek clearly chose the word *anthropos* to describe the incarnation of the Son of God (the second hypostasis/ person of the Trinity). The creed says in Greek, "...who for us *anthropous* [men, i. e. human beings] became man [*enanthropesanta*]. We might say in English that He was "anthropized," though fortunately such a strange word was avoided. When we say, then, that Christ "became man," we mean that He took upon himself the human nature that is common to both men and women, though He Himself was a male human being. He did this "for us men," that is, for all of us who are human beings, both male and female.

The statement concerning the Holy Spirit follows the original formulation of the second ecumenical council that the Holy Spirit "proceeds from the Father." In order to combat the Arian heresy, the Western Church later added the word *Filioque*, ("and the Son," that is, "the Spirit proceeds from the Father and the Son") so that there would be no doubt that the Father and the Son are one God and equal "hypostases/persons." The intention of the original council was to define the Holy Spirit as one hypostasis/person, and one in divinity with the Father and the Son, as the creed says, "together with the Father and the Son he is worshiped and glorified." To do this, the Fathers appealed to the Bible, and took a phrase from the Gospel of St. John, "When the Advocate comes, whom I will send you from the Father, the Spirit of truth that proceeds from the Father, he will testify to me" (John 15:26). In view of this, the Byzantine Churches in communion with Rome use the original form of the Creed. In 2003, after several years of dialogue, the North American Orthodox-Catholic Theological Consultation, sponsored by the Catholic and Orthodox bishops, issued an Agreed Statement, *The Filioque: A Church-Dividing Issue?* After a lengthy summary of the question, it made a series of recommendations, including the following: "…that the Catholic Church, as a consequence of the normative and irrevocable dogmatic value of the Creed of 381, use the original Greek text alone in making translations of that Creed for catechetical and liturgical use."

The Dialogue Introducing the Anaphora

The most important prayer in the Divine Liturgy is the anaphora, or "prayer of offering." The priest says this prayer in the name of the whole community, but we all offer it together after preparing ourselves in the grace of God as best we can in faith and love for one another. Therefore, at this point the deacon, who has the role of guiding the celebration of the Divine Liturgy, announces solemnly, "Let us stand aright, let us stand in awe, let us be attentive to offer the holy offering in peace."

At this point in the Liturgy, we are already standing so here the deacon is asking us to stand "straight," and "with attentiveness." This calls us to more than just physical standing, but a standing in the faith, for God has raised us up and we are no longer "bent over." In fact, the general posture for prayer in the early was to stand; sitting was never a posture of prayer. There were no pews in church, and the only ones who sat were the bishop and presbyters, because sitting was the sign of presiding. For example, kings would sit to proclaim laws or pronouncements, while everyone else stood.

Customs, of course, have changed. In the second century, Origen indicated that people prayed sitting when they could not physically stand. Modern humanity seems to be more concerned about comfort. Certainly, services should not be a test of endurance, but there is no need to sit as much as possible. We should stand when a prayer with a doxology is being said, especially for the anaphora. The prayer of the priest is our prayer, which we make our own by saying "Amen."

Kneeling is also ancient to Christianity. St. Paul knelt to pray (Acts 20:36; 21:5). Kneeling is a sign of our humility before God. We are fallen, we are sinful; we can be lifted up only by God. Kneeling, then, is a sign of penance, humility and supplication. Standing is an act of faith in the presence of God in His resurrection: that in the anaphora and through Communion He can raise us to stand upright. Canon 20 of the Council of Nicea prescribed that people should always pray standing on Sundays and daily from Pascha to Pentecost as a sign of our faith in the resurrection. The custom of kneeling during some parts of the anaphora was adopted from the Latin rite.

The deacon also says, "let us stand in awe." The word "awe" is used here to translate the Greek word *phobos*, which also means "fear." We see this in words such as "claustrophobia" (a fear of closed places) and "acrophobia"(a fear of heights). There are healthy and unhealthy forms of fear. We should not have such a fear of God that we are paralyzed from seeking to do good. However, we need the kind of fear that makes us recognize our dependence on God, who alone is good and who alone can bring us to salvation. Therefore, the Book of Proverbs tells us, "The fear of the Lord is the beginning of wisdom" (Proverbs 1:7) and St. Paul writes, "Work out your salvation with fear and trembling" (Philippians 2:12). A healthy fear makes us take our faith seriously, though we might tend to prefer a more comfortable Christianity.

The deacon then says, "let us be attentive to offer the holy Anaphora in peace." Here the word for "offering" is "anaphora" and refers directly to the prayer that is about to be said. The people respond, "Mercy, peace, a sacrifice of praise," a very difficult phrase to translate. It is not a complete sentence, but a kind of acclamation, meaning that the anaphora is mercy, is peace, is a sacrifice of praise. It reminds us of Matthew 9:13, where our Lord says, "What I desire is mercy, not sacrifice." Christ denounced empty sacrifices, without an internal spirit of love. After the death and resurrection of Christ, all earlier sacrifices have been made obsolete. The mercy demanded by the Lord and the true sacrifice of praise are identical: the Divine Liturgy which we celebrate now by His command. The Divine Liturgy is the perfect sacrifice: a sacrifice of praise offered to God out of love. It is the peace that comes to us from above, since the Eucharistic offering is Christ, "who is our peace, [and] who made both one and broke down the dividing wall of enmity through his flesh" (Ephesians 2:14): the peace of reconciliation between God and humanity that unites both is Communion.

The constant teaching of the universal Church is that the Divine Liturgy is the one sacrifice of Christ now offered in a mystical way. The whole mystery of His life from the incarnation of the Word of God, to His death on the cross, His resurrection and His glorification are truly present in the Liturgy. The Liturgy remembers the historical sacrifice of our Lord — the whole paschal mystery of death and resurrection — in such a way that the reality of what was accomplished is present, in an unbloody manner in our sacrifice of praise. This whole reality of God's love for us — His giving Himself to us and we to Him — and His gift of redemption and sanctification are dynamically active in the Liturgy in the present. The sacrifice of Christ, not bloody but unbloody, not historical but mystical; is really and fully present in our liturgical celebration.

The "sacrifice of praise" is more than mere words. Our glorification of the paschal mystery indicates our acceptance of it in mind and will, and the integration of this mystery into our own lives. It is our assimilation into this mystery, as St. Paul wrote, "I urge you, therefore, brothers, by the mercies of God, to offer your bodies as a living sacrifice, holy and pleasing to God, your spiritual worship" (Romans 12:1).

Besides being a commemoration and a re-presentation of Christ's sacrifice here and now, there is a dimension to the Liturgy which is sometimes obscured or lost, but which was emphasized by the earlier Fathers, particularly St Maximos the Confessor. The Liturgy is a prophecy and foretaste of what is yet to come. The future Kingdom, the fulfillment of all things is already present in the reality of the Liturgy.

After the deacon's greeting, the priest pronounces a blessing taken from 2 Corinthians 13:13, "The grace of our Lord Jesus Christ, and the love of God and Father and the communion of the Holy Spirit, be with all of you." The Liturgy adds to the original scriptural formula the Trinitarian clarification, the love of God "the Father." Undoubtedly the most ancient form of this greeting was the simpler, "Peace be to all." The current blessing was first found in the writings of Theodore of Mopsuestia, St. John Chrysostom's schoolmate in Syria (Homily 16, 2). From then on it has been the opening dialogue of the Byzantine anaphora, which is addressed to God the Father, commemorating and fulfilling the command of the incarnate Son, in the power of the Holy Spirit.

What do we mean when we say "The Lord is with us?" In the Divine Liturgy God acts through His Holy Spirit. The bread and wine we are about to offer will truly become in substance the body and blood of Christ. However, not simply like some "stuff" we receive that does not change us, it is God living in us and enabling us to do His work. God shows Himself in the way we act and what we accomplish. He creates among us a community capable of transforming the world so that the Christian community is a fellowship "full of the Holy Spirit," of the power and love of God.

Our response to the priest, "And with your spirit," does not mean simply, "And with you." The Fathers' commentaries inter-pret it in the sense of the gift of the Holy Spirit that is present to the priest ordained by the grace of the Spirit. With the understanding of the Lord with us as the presence of the Spirit, the power of God in the community, this response is natural and makes perfect sense.

The dialogue continues with the ancient phrase, "Let us lift up our hearts," which in Greek is very simple, "Up with the hearts." Our response is "we lift them up to the Lord." This simple exchange must be very ancient, because it is found in all Christian liturgies. The original meaning was probably to put aside all earthly cares, to direct our attention to the Lord who is above, as in Colossians 3:1-2, "If ... you were raised with Christ, seek what is above, where Christ is seated at the right hand of God. Think of what is above, not of what is on earth." The antiquity of the saying probably means that the priest and the people may have here lifted their hands in prayer. The second-century writer, Tertullian, even notes that the Christians were laughed at as being "cloud counters" because they prayed with hands raised. Today the priest still raises his hands at this point.

The priest concludes the dialogue saying, "Let us give thanks to the Lord," and the people respond, "It is proper and just." Again, this is an ancient exchange used in all Christian Churches. The phrase "...to worship the Father, and the Son and the Holy Spirit, the Trinity one in substance and undivided" was added to the Slavonic Liturgy in the seventeenth century because the priest prayed the first part of the anaphora silently. Today it is being removed to allow for the public recitation of the prayer.

When he says, "let us give thanks," the priest is actually asking the permission of the congregation to continue: "Should we give thanks to the Lord?" The people respond, "Yes," or more formally, "It is proper and right." The priest then accepts the people's permission and continues, "It is truly proper and right..." The response itself is one of those popular acclamations common in ancient times. Even today, we use some popular acclamations when we are gathered in groups, like, "Hear, hear," or "He's a jolly good fellow," and others. The Latin form of this response was used at the election of an emperor. When his name was announced to the crowds, they would respond, "It is right, it is just." When the people have given their consent, then, the priest begins the anaphora, the solemn prayer of thanksgiving of the Divine Liturgy.

Beginning of the Anaphora: We Give Thanks

The most important prayer of the Divine Liturgy is certainly the anaphora, or prayer of offering. Sometimes we may have a false idea that the anaphora is simply something the priest does and the people watch. It is, however, a corporate act of the whole community, and as I continue this commentary, we will see that the congregation has quite an active role in the anaphora. St. John Chrysostom could not be more clear that it is a prayer of both the priest and the people:

> "One sees that the people contribute much to the prayer... during the fearful mysteries, the priest speaks for the people, and the people speak on behalf of the priest, as can be seen from these words, 'And with your spirit.' The prayer of thanksgiving is again a common prayer offered by the priest and by all the people. The priest begins, and the people join him and respond that it is just and right to praise God: this is the beginning of the thanksgiving. Why are you surprised if the people mix their voice with that of the priest? Do you not know that these holy hymns rise to the heavens, where they mixed with those of the angels, the cherubim and the heavenly powers?" (Homily 18 on 1 Corinthians)

"To give thanks" was the best Greek attempt to translate the Hebrew word *berekah*, a much more general word meaning, "to praise, to glorify, to bless, to thank, to proclaim the greatness." The anaphora always begins with one of these words, all of which are attempts to translate the Hebrew original. It conveys a sense of acknowledgment of all God's works, an acceptance of His acts of love, and our offering and consecration of ourselves to Him in return. Anaphoras written in Greek usually attempt to express these ideas with a string of words all trying to express the Hebrew completely. Therefore, in the Divine Liturgy of St. John Chrysostom, we begin the anaphora, "It is proper and just to bless you, to praise you, to thank you, to worship you..."

In this first part of the prayer, we, as human beings, attempt to do what is beyond human powers: to give an adequate thanksgiving to God who has brought us into being "out of nonexistence," who sustains us in being and brings us to the future kingdom where we will be together with God. We are overwhelmed by the love that God has poured out upon us, and we strain to express our thanksgiving by word piled upon word, which yet remains inadequate. Like St. Paul, we cry out, "Neither death, nor life, nor angels, nor principalities, nor present things, nor future things, nor power, nor height, nor depth, nor any other creature will be able to separate us from the love of God in Christ Jesus our Lord" (Romans 8:38-39). For this reason, we "bless, praise, thank and worship" God, who is "ineffable, inconceivable, invisible, incomprehensible, ever existing yet ever the same." John the Theologian wrote, "No one has ever seen God. The only Son, God, who is at the Father's side, has revealed him" (John 1:18). God's presence to us is more essential than the air we breathe, providing for our lives from the beginning of creation to the fulfillment of our destiny. Therefore, we thank Him "for all that we know and that we do not know, for the manifest and hidden benefits bestowed on us."

In this first part of the anaphora, we try to adequately thank God for all the blessings of creation, too many to be counted and beyond our comprehension. Of course, we cannot thank Him adequately unless the priest says these words aloud for our hearing. To read them silently in a book is to suppress the proclamation we make as a community through the mouth of the priest. It also explains why the ordained priest must read the prayer aloud. Not only does it make the proclamation more clear by avoiding the "babel" of many voices, but the words uttered are beyond human understanding and said by one who has received the gift of the Holy Spirit in ordination for this task. The Anaphora of St. Basil asks, "Who is able to proclaim your might, to make known all your praises, or to recount all your mighty deeds in every age?" It is the priest, praying in the Spirit, on behalf of the people.

The first part of the Anaphora of St. Basil is quite different, but, like that of St. John Chrysostom, it also piles word upon word in an attempt to express what God has done for us. Here we "praise, hymn, bless, worship, thank, and glorify" God. The anaphoras are addressed to God the Father. To express our faith in the Trinity, the Anaphora of St. John Chrysostom makes clear that when we glorify the Father, we also glorify the Son and the Spirit, one in essence with the Father. By praying in this way, we fulfill the promise of our Lord at the Last Supper, "I will tell you clearly about the Father... On that day you will ask in my name, and I do not tell you that I ask the Father for you" (John 16:15-16). When we pray, therefore, we pray to God, to the Father through the Son and in the Holy Spirit (cf. the doxology for the prayer at the bowing of heads). The Anaphora of St. Basil expresses the unity of the Trinity by our prayer to the Father "of our great God, Savior and Lord Jesus Christ, ... through whom the Holy Spirit has been revealed." Here title is piled upon title in a desperate attempt to adequately describe God. Jesus is "our hope, the image of the Father's goodness, the seal bearing the Father's likeness, the Living Word, True God, Eternal Wisdom, Life, Sanctification, Power and the True Light," all images take from Holy Scripture. The Spirit, too, is "the Spirit of Truth, the gift of Filial Adoption, the Pledge of our Future Inheritance, the Firstfruits of Eternal Blessings, the Life-creating Power, and the wellspring of Sanctification."

The first part of either anaphora is a glorification of all God has done for us. However, I have heard people object that we cannot "glorify" God. It is true that all glory in heaven and on earth belongs to God, and that we cannot, as creatures, add to the glory of God. Yet, we have been created in the image of God, and so in all creation we alone can recognize and acknowledge that all glory belongs to God. It is in this sense that we glorify God. We are professing that "All glory [belongs] to God." Jesus prays then for us, "And I have given them the glory you gave me, so that they may be one, as we are one" (John 17:22).

Before we move on, another misconception must be mentioned. In the Roman Mass, the corresponding prayer is not a part of the traditional Eucharistic Canon. It could vary with the occasion or feast or season, and so was not considered a part of the canon, and thus was called the "preface." Sometimes, because we have been trained in Roman Catholic schools, or have been influenced by Roman Catholic liturgical theology, we might think the prayer of thanksgiving not to be part of the anaphora. However, in the Byzantine tradition, the anaphora essentially includes this first part of the prayer.

The Hymn of Victory

The priest introduces a new theme in the anaphora by saying, "We also thank you for this liturgy which you are pleased to accept from our hands, even though there stand before you thousands of archangels, tens of thousands of angels, cherubim and seraphim, six-winged, many-eyed, soaring aloft on their wings, singing, shouting, crying aloud and saying the triumphal hymn." The Anaphora of St. Basil is even more elaborate and lists the nine choirs of angelic powers here.

From this introduction, we take the name of this hymn, the "triumphal hymn," or the "hymn of victory." The four words introducing the hymn are ultimately from the prophecy of Ezekiel 1:10-12, where four living creatures surround God's throne where He resides in glory. Therefore, the eagle sings, the lion shouts, the ox cries out and the man says (speaks).

The people then respond by proclaiming that God is holy. Holiness itself is a transcendent goodness, beyond human capabilities, a gift of God. Since all that is good comes from God, He is above all holy beyond our power to comprehend. Just as the priest must struggle to express goodness in creation, so the people try to respond to that gift with a three-fold confession of God's holiness: "Holy, holy, holy...." for a single simple proclamation of God's holiness would not suffice.

We see here that while the anaphora is a single prayer concluding with an "Amen," it is also divided into sections, which might technically be called strophes, which is Greek for "a turning," or "a twist." The words of the priest declare God's love directed toward His people; the hymn of the people "turns" back to God to confess His "otherness," His "holiness."

The origin of this text is Isaiah's heavenly vision of God's throne in heaven: "I saw the Lord seated on a high and lofty throne, with the train of his garment filling the temple. Seraphim were stationed above; each of them had six wings; with two they veiled their faces, with two they veiled the feet, and with two they hovered aloft. 'Holy, holy, holy is the Lord of hosts!' they cried out one to the other. 'All the earth is filled with his glory!' At the sound of that cry, the frame of the door shook and the house was filled with smoke" (Isaiah 6:2-4). The Christian Liturgy adds heaven to earth. In this way, the prophet's vision of the majesty and holiness of God is made a part of our worship. We see the presence of God through the eyes of the mystery of faith.

The hymn of victory also unites our worship to the angelic glorification of God in heaven. Our Liturgy on earth is a mystical representation of the heavenly angelic worship. Their presence is invoked in the prayer of the little entrance and our ministry is likened to theirs in the Cherubikon. This symbolism points to something real: the Liturgy indeed unites us with transcendent glorification. If the Liturgy were just for this world, it would be a hopeless exercise; it could not possibly deliver what it promises. It would be an empty promise, and meaningless words and gestures. When we are unable to grasp spiritual symbols, the Liturgy does become meaningless. Likewise, if the Liturgy were simply a heavenly, spiritual reality, with no relationship to our lives on earth and justice among peoples and nations, then it would also be meaningless, a flight from reality, a haven from the turmoil of the world. Angels, however, are the connection, or, to put it better, the symbolic reality of the connection. Our concept of angels may be symbolic, but it makes concrete the abstract notion of the union of earthly and heavenly realities that gives the Liturgy its force to actually and truly change human life. In our own time, the Passion is in the past, but Christ is enthroned with the Father and the past is truly as present now as well as the future. The angels, therefore, symbolize eternity and freedom from all bonds of space and time.

In a subtle way, which is always more effective, this angelic vision is then brought into our history and into our space. We sing

"Blessed is he who comes in the name of the Lord. Hosanna in the highest." The Hebrew *Hosanna* means "Save us, we pray" — the acclamation of the people welcoming Jesus into Jerusalem, seated upon the donkey's foal as upon the cherubic throne in the heavens — and is united to Isaiah's vision. The first part of the hymn of victory corresponds to the first section of the anaphora, which speaks of God's goodness and holiness. The second part looks forward to the next section of the anaphora, which will tell the story of our salvation in Christ.

The Anaphora Continues: Giving Thanks for Christ

After the people sing the hymn of victory, the priest proclaims the next part of the anaphora. We turn to God's work of salvation accomplished through the incarnation, that is, the act of the Son and Word of God becoming a human being, Jesus, the Son of Mary. To Him was given the title, "Messiah," the "Christ," the "Anointed One." That is why we sing, "Blessed is he who comes in the name of the Lord."

This part of the anaphora tells of God's self-revelation to us. This fact of revelation is the center of the message of Christ. The Epistle to the Hebrews begins, "In times past, God spoke in partial and various ways to our ancestors through the prophets; in these last days [that is, the time in which we live, from Christ until now], he spoke to us through a son, whom he made heir of all things and through whom he created the universe, who is the refulgence of his glory, the very imprint of his being, and who sustains all things by his mighty word" (Hebrews 1:1-3). The importance of revelation, of God manifesting Himself to us is also emphasized in the beginning of the Gospel of St. John, where Jesus the Word of God is proclaimed to be the fulfillment of all revelation, particularly the Law of Moses. "This life was the light of the world, the light shines in the darkness, and the darkness has not overcome it.... and the Word became flesh and made his dwelling among us, and we saw his glory, the glory of the Father's only Son, full of grace and truth ... From his fullness we have all received, grace in place of grace, because while the law was given through Moses, grace and truth came through Jesus Christ" (John 1:4-5, 14, 16-17). Note that God's revelation is not just empty words, but is full of action, making us holy and alive. God is "the Giver of Life, the Savior of our souls, the Lover of Humankind," titles that are repeated over and over again in the Liturgy.

This section of the anaphora is based on a passage from the Gospel of St. John, "God so loved the world that he gave his only Son, so that everyone who believes in him might not perish but might have eternal life" (John 3:16). In the Anaphora of St. John Chrysostom, this passage from the Gospels summarizes everything that Christ has done for us, and the drama of salvation is not recounted in detail. Instead, the anaphora observes, "He [Jesus] came and fulfilled the whole divine plan in our behalf," and then goes to the climax at the Last Supper.

What is said in summary form and very simply in the Anaphora of St. John Chrysostom is described in greater detail in the Anaphora of St. Basil. St. Basil, who was probably the author of the anaphora in its final form, wove together a tapestry of texts from the New Testament, particularly the Epistles of St. Paul, to tell the story of God's salvation for the assembly of Christians gathered for worship. This anaphora, then, corresponds more exactly to the Jewish Seder meal, which recounted the passing of the Israelites through the Red Sea by the power of God, so escaping slavery in Egypt. Here it is Christ, who, through His passage through the womb of Mary, through His emptying of Himself (Greek, *kenosis*) on the cross, condemned "sin in His flesh, so that those who died in Adam [all of us] might be brought to life in Him." We see in greater detail God's love for the world, for "He freed us from Death's despair and rose on the third day, preparing the way for the resurrection of all flesh from the dead."

In the Anaphora of St. Basil, we see clearly why every Liturgy is a memorial of our Lord's resurrection. We can also understand why the Liturgy of St. Basil was the primary Eucharist of the Byzantine Church, and was celebrated on feast days and all Sundays. It is the Church's proclamation of God's revelation and of His plan of salvation, which the Liturgy of St. John Chrysostom summarized in the simple words, "You so loved your world that you gave your only-begotten Son."

The Anaphora: the Institution Narrative

The narrative part of the holy anaphoras of St. John Chrysostom and St. Basil the Great both end with the story of the Last (Mystical) Supper of our Lord with His disciples, when Jesus "took bread into His holy and all-pure and immaculate hands, gave thanks and blessed, sanctified, broke and gave it to His holy disciples and apostles." The giving of this bread and cup of wine becomes for us the presence of God in our midst as Redeemer and Sanctifier "until the end of the age" (Matthew 28:20). The climax of the narration of God's saving deeds is the institution of the Eucharist.

It seems now that the most ancient Eucharistic prayers did not necessarily include the words of our Lord, "This is my body," and "This is my blood," although they were added very early to emphasize the fact that our Divine Liturgy is a memorial of what our Lord did at the Mystical Supper to reveal that He would be with us always and that His body and blood would be given in Communion under the form of bread and wine. It also seems that the words of institution ("This is my body," "This is my blood") were added into the anaphoras in a standard form, which we might now call its fourth part, or fourth strophe. These words of our Lord have achieved a special status in our prayer. Even in the Byzantine rite, they were always pronounced aloud by the priest with great reverence, and the people reaffirm them by singing "Amen" ("So be it").

In the Western tradition, these words are called the "consecration," and have been sometimes considered by Roman theologians as the moment of change of the bread and wine. However, the Anaphora of the Holy Apostles Addai and Mari in the Church of the East (the Assyrian/Chaldean Church) is an exception, for it does not contain the words of institution at all. The Roman Catholic Church has recently (October 26, 2001) made the determination that, because of its antiquity, the Anaphora of Addai and

Mari is a true prayer of consecration even without the words of our Lord.

There is a slight variation in the Gospels in the words Jesus used for the cup. In the Gospel of St. Luke (22:20) and the first letter of St. Paul to the Corinthians 11:25, the tradition is, "This cup is the new covenant in my blood." This tradition is followed by the Roman Church. In the Gospels of St. Matthew (26:28) and of St. Mark (14:24) the words are "This is my blood of the covenant." This tradition is followed by the Byzantine Churches. It is clear, however, that both versions mean the same thing: that by shedding His blood on the cross for our life and salvation, the Son and Word of God was making a New Covenant with the human race. He died for us that we might live and commit ourselves totally to God by loving Him with our whole heart and mind and soul and loving one another as He has loved us.

In the theology of John Chrysostom, Christ's words at the Last Supper are like the words of creation: "It is not man that converts the holy gifts into the body and blood of Christ, but Christ Himself, who gave Himself to be crucified. The priest, who utters these words, is only an image of Christ, but the power and grace are from God. He says: 'This is my body.' These words change the sacrificial elements. Just as the words: 'Increase and multiply and fill the earth' (Gen 1:28) although spoken once, give our nature the permanent power of procreation; so also these words once pronounced, are effective on all the altars from that time until now and will be to His second coming."

St. John Chrysostom tells us that these words of our Lord, spoken at the Last Supper, affect the created gifts of bread and wine for all time, making them the presence of God among us in the Divine Liturgy. The priest is not a magician. He only repeats the words of Christ for the remembrance of the people. The real change occurs through the power of God who works through His Holy Spirit. When God acts in our behalf, the Trinity is always involved. It is the Father who sent the Son into the world in the incarnation and the Spirit into the Church, the Son who speaks the words of revelation, "This is my body," and "This is my blood," and the Spirit as the power of God who fulfills the plan of God.

St. John Chrysostom is not talking about the moment when the gifts change. He is speaking instead about how the words that Christ said reverberate throughout time to effect the change in a manner similar to creation. The priest "stands in the place of Christ" when he says these words, for the individual presbyter obviously does not mean that the bread is his body, but the body of Christ. The priest is a passive instrument of God in all the sacramental mysteries, so in the Byzantine liturgical tradition sacramental words are always in the passive voice, as in baptism, "The servant of God is baptized....". For the early Fathers, when the entire anaphora, which is the prayer for the consecration of the gifts, had been said, the bread and wine had become the body and blood of Christ. The instant in which this happens is not as important as our faith that "Christ is present whole and entire in each of the species [the bread and wine] and whole and entire in each of their parts" (*Catechism of the Catholic Church*, § 1377).

It is important to remember that the Liturgy is the commemoration, remembrance, and calling to mind of the saving work of Christ. It is quite appropriate to tell the story of the Lord's Supper, the first meal at which this "remembrance" was done, the breaking of bread in which we recognize Jesus connecting it to the presence of Christ, although the Liturgy is not a dramatic re-enactment of the Last Supper. They do not only convey the truth of the presence of Jesus, but also of the action by which these gifts save us. His body is "broken for you," His blood is "shed for you and for many, for the remission (forgiveness) of sins." All forgiveness and reconciliation flow from the sacrifice of our Lord commemorated in the Divine Liturgy. It is for all these reasons that the words pronounced originally by our Lord, God and Savior Jesus Christ have such an important role in the Divine Liturgy.

The Anaphora: the Anamnesis

The story of the wondrous works God has done in our behalf concludes with the narration of the Last Supper. Here Christ revealed the mystical and sacramental way in which He would keep

His promise to remain with us until the end of time and commanded us, "Do this in memory of me." In the Anaphora of St. Basil, after the people's "Amen," the priest continues, "Do this in remembrance of me. For as often as you eat this bread and drink this chalice, you proclaim my death and profess my resurrection." This command of our Lord is proclaimed in the Anaphora of St. Basil, but for some reason is only alluded to in the Anaphora of St. John Chrysostom. Perhaps this phrase dropped out of the Liturgy at some point.

In both anaphoras the priest continues, "Therefore, O Master, we also remember his saving passion, the life-giving cross, the three days in the tomb, the resurrection from the dead, the ascension into heaven, the enthronement at your right hand, God and Father and finally his glorious and fearsome second coming." This is called, in Greek, the *anamnesis*, which means the commemoration.

The anamnesis of the Liturgy is based on Holy Scripture, the Bible. It is the word of God in action. St. Paul describes the Last Supper, the mystical supper of our Lord, and then observes, "for as often as you eat this bread and drink the cup, you proclaim the death of the Lord until he comes" (1 Corinthians 11:26). It is clear that St. Paul here is speaking about the death of the Lord as His saving action. In Philippians 2:8-9 we read, "[Christ Jesus] humbled himself, becoming obedient to death, even death on a cross. Because of this, God greatly exalted him and bestowed on him the name that is above every other name." The glory of Jesus is His resurrection, and so, for Christians, to glorify the cross is to proclaim the resurrection. The ancient commemoration was expanded to include the resurrection so that our faith would be clear in this matter. As the anaphora developed, then, all of God's saving deeds were added — the ascension, the enthronement, even the "coming again" in glory — because since God has promised this and He is eternal, outside of time, it has in a way already happened. It is especially because of the anamnesis (the "commemoration") that the anaphora is considered the real presence of the mystery of the resurrection, and is not said on weekdays of the Great Fast.

The anamnesis is a remembering, but not in the sense of a simple "calling to mind." It is a sacrificial memorial, in the Christian sense of a "sacrifice of praise," in which the bloody sacrifice of the cross is really present in an unbloody praise or glorification. St. John Chrysostom said, "Do we not offer daily? Certainly we offer thus, making an anamnesis of His death. How is it one and not many? Because it was offered once, like that which was carried into the holy of holies.... For we ever offer the same Person, not today one sheep and next time a different one, but ever the same offering. Therefore the sacrifice is one. By this argument, then, since the offering is made in many places, does it follow that there are many Christs? Not at all, for Christ is everywhere one, complete here and complete there, a single body. Thus, as when offered in many places He is one body and not many bodies, so also there is one sacrifice. One High Priest is He who offered the sacrifice which cleanses us. We offer even now that which was then offered, which cannot be exhausted. This is done for an anamnesis of that which was then done, for 'do this' He said 'for the anamnesis of me.' We do not offer a different sacrifice like the high-priest of old, but we ever offer the same. Or rather we offer the anamnesis of the sacrifice" (Homily on Hebrews 17,3). The anamnesis, then, is an explicit expression of what the whole anaphora is: the commemoration of God's salvation, which is real because God remembers as we also remember.

The Anaphora: the Offering

If the Divine Liturgy is to be the sacrifice of our Lord, it must also include an offering. The act of offering is essential to the very core of the Liturgy. This is why the central prayer is called the anaphora, the prayer of offering. However, the act of offering is expressed in many different ways in the Liturgies of the various Churches. In the Roman Liturgy there is an act of offering in the anaphora, which is called the Eucharistic prayer in the West. There is also a second ritual outside of the anaphora called the offertory, which is performed by the priest after the gifts of bread and wine are brought to the holy table. I mention this because sometimes people have claimed that there must be a similar offertory somewhere in the Byzantine rite also because it is "essential" to the Liturgy. It is true that the Liturgy, as a sacrifice, must be offered; but the essential offering is what is done within the anaphora itself, when the deacon lifts up the diskos and chalice containing the holy gifts while the priest prays, chanting, "...offering You Your own from Your own."

At first, this wording might strike us as somewhat unusual. Why do we not simply say, "We offer to you?" It is because the act of offering is a part of a continuous act of "remembering," and "offering" and "entreating," that is done together in the Spirit of God. The concrete action that we do is to "praise," to "bless," to "thank" and to "pray," while together with God we are remembering and offering the holy gifts. In other words, the central action of the Liturgy is our prayer to the Father that the offering of the Liturgy be accomplished. It is here, then, that we enter into the heart of the mystery of the Liturgy, and the words that are used are simple yet profound.

The words that the priest says while the gesture of offering is made by the deacon — who here represents the whole congregation, signifying that the offering is made by all those present — is really a Greek triple conceptual word play. The Greeks loved words and always found different layers of meaning in them. These words of offering can be understood on several levels:

- First, since the bread and wine are created elements, we offer to God what He himself has created;

- Second, since the bread and wine are becoming the body and blood of Christ, we offer to God His only Son, whom He has given for the life of the world; and

- Third, since we eat the created gifts, we are also united with the uncreated Son in the uncreated Holy Spirit, so that we become "God's own," and so offer what we are ourselves becoming.

In addition, it should be noted that the gifts we offer are not the raw gifts of wheat and grapes from nature, but the "artificial" gifts of bread and wine that have already been transformed by our labor, so that we are offering to God the work of our hands. In the same way, the Eucharist is truly the Body of Christ, but it is also us, for we form the Church, which is the Body of Christ (see Ephesians 1:22-23).

The offering takes the Eucharist out of historical time, and brings it into the eternal mystery of God that is being brought to fulfillment. In the Gospel of Luke, therefore, we find Jesus say, "Happy is he who eats bread in the kingdom of God" (Luke 14:15). The cup, overflowing with abundance, is also a symbol of future fullness.

"Offering you your own from your own," are among the most ancient liturgical words. The question has been raised by some that perhaps "Yours of your own," refers not to the Eucharistic gifts, but to other charitable gifts that were also offered simultaneously at the Liturgy. The reason for this opinion is that what immediately follows is, "Moreover, we offer you this spiritual and unbloody sacrifice," as if it were distinct from the first offering. However, in the second century, in the works of St. Irenaeus, we already find these words being applied to the Eucharist, "For we offer to God His own, announcing consistently the fellowship and union of the flesh and Spirit. For, as the bread, which is produced from the earth, when it receives the invocation of God, is no longer common bread, but the Eucharist, consisting of two realities, earthly and heavenly; so also our bodies, when they receive the Eucharist, are no longer corruptible, having the hope of the resurrection to eternity." If the gifts of bread and wine are being transformed in the banquet to which Christ calls us through the power of His Holy Spirit, then we, too, who are about to partake of this meal, are also being transformed. We cannot take part in the Divine Liturgy without being changed. When we offer God "His own," we also become "His own," because the offering is done not simply with human hands or human heart, but in the Spirit of God present in our hearts and souls.

If someone attends the Liturgy as a matter of rote, or from the burden of obligation, and resists the action of God who is present, then there is a risk of the danger of St. Paul's warning to the

Corinthians, "Whoever eats the bread and drinks the cup of the Lord unworthily will have to answer for the body and blood of the Lord" (1 Corinthians 11:27). What this means practically is that when we offer to God the sacrifice of the body and blood of our Lord, our food in Holy Communion, we must also offer our very selves. In offering the Liturgy we accomplish what St. Paul tells us to do, "I urge you therefore, brothers, by the mercies of God, to offer your bodies as a living sacrifice holy and pleasing to God, your spiritual worship" (Romans 12:1).

The Anaphora: "We Praise You"

The anaphora is not a prayer said by the priest alone as he stands at the holy table. The people interrupt him at many points, such as at the hymn of victory. This should not be surprising, because the anaphora is the prayer of the whole Church. Though the priest reads it aloud, the people join in occasionally with enthusiasm. This is why it doesn't make sense for the priest to hide the words from the people. Now that the Liturgy is in the vernacular, the full theology of our prayer can be proclaimed for the hearing of all. The fact that the people respond so frequently during the anaphora shows that it is not the exclusive prayer of the priest.

Perhaps the most important intervention of the people is the hymn, "We praise you, we bless you, we thank you, O Lord, and we pray to you, our God." This hymn summarizes the whole anaphora and, expresses the congregation's involvement in the whole action of thanksgiving. The words "praise, bless, thank" and "pray," are the action verbs on which our remembrance, our offering of the holy gifts and our invoking of the Holy Spirit depends. To speak grammatically, "praise, bless, thank and pray" are the finite verbs and "remembering," and "offering" are participles depending on them. This hymn shows that the people have a direct role in the crucial and most important part of the anaphora. Together "we praise, bless and thank" God, as we remember His works of salvation, as we offer up the gifts of bread and wine that become the body and blood of Christ, and as we ask

God to send down the Holy Spirit to sanctify us and the gifts.

The hymn itself is divided into two sections. The first part — we "praise, bless and thank"— refers to what we have already done while "we pray" refers to what we are about to do. As we have seen, the priest began the anaphora with a series of five verbs, "It is proper and just to sing to you, to bless you, to praise you, to thank you, to worship you," all expressing aspects of the Hebrew concept, *berekah*. Three of these words are repeated in this hymn. This is what we have done. We have praised God because He has created all that there is in His love for our very existence and He has remained faithful to us even after we sinned. We bless God, who in His infinite wisdom, loved the world so much that He sent His only Son, that we "should not perish, but have life everlasting." We thank God for the gift of our Lord Jesus Christ, who has "blessed, sanctified, broken and given" us His body and blood in the Eucharist. Therefore, remembering all these works of salvation, and we also enumerate the cross, the tomb, the resurrection, the ascension, the sitting at the right hand and the second coming in glory, and offering the gifts created by God for our salvation, we "praise, bless and thank" the Lord.

Then follows the conjunction "and," which here turns us towards what we are about to do. Prayer in the strict sense (supplication) means asking God for something. We must not look down on "begging" God for a blessing. Sometimes we exalt ourselves too much to see the reality that exists between God and ourselves. Indeed, much of primitive Christian prayer was asking God for things, and intercessory prayer has persisted in our daily offices to this day. In the Liturgy, we are about to ask God to send the Holy Spirit to make us holy through the gifts that become, through His power, the instrument of our union with God in Communion. Because of this divine action, our worship is more than supplication; it is also transformation. The Liturgy is communication with God, in which not only an exchange of information takes place, but we are ourselves transformed into the divine image. God becomes our Father, our Brother and our Sanctifier. The Russian theologian and saint Ignatius Brianchaninov wrote, "When prayer seizes people, it transforms them progressively, making them spiritual from their union with the Holy Spirit." In the Divine Liturgy, the Holy Spirit takes hold of us through Communion.

There is a difficulty we face in translating this hymn. The priest introduces the hymn, "We praise you..." with a formula that has been translated "on behalf of all and for all." The meaning of this phrase is not completely clear. It belongs to the most ancient texts of the Liturgy, where succinct vocabulary was the rule. Earlier, sentences were short and to the point, later on we tended to become long-winded. We usually attach the phrase in question to the priest's proclamation of our offering, "offering you yours of your own," which we explained previously. However, if we compare this passage to other liturgies, both Eastern and Western, we find that this phrase clearly belongs to the hymn that follows. We don't know if it was actually sung by the people, for it may have been a lead-in by the priest, but it does belong to what follows. An analysis of the words in Greek also shows that this phrase may be interpreted adverbially, that is, indicating the circumstances in which our praise is given. They can have a local and temporal meaning. Therefore, the phrase could mean: "In all times and places we praise you, we bless you, we glorify you..." equivalent to the Latin *semper et ubique* ("always and everywhere"). It would seem then that the sense of this hymn is, "Always and everywhere we praise you, we bless you, we thank you, O Lord, and we pray to you, our God." This is significant, for the early Church saw our Eucharistic sacrifice as the true fulfillment of the Old Testament prophecy of Malachy: "For from the rising of the sun, even to its setting [that is, "always"], my name is great among the nations [praised, blessed and thanked); and everywhere they bring sacrifice to my name, and a pure offering, for great is my name among the nations, says the Lord of Hosts" (Malachy 1:11).

The Anaphora: the Epiklesis

After the congregation sings this hymn, the priest begins to pray in the name of the community, "We implore, pray and entreat" the

Father to send the Holy Spirit upon us and upon the gifts being offered. In Greek, this invocation is called the epiklesis, which means literally, a "calling upon." It is the climax of the anaphora, which follows the three-fold Jewish pattern of prayer used by our Lord. We address God; we commemorate His blessings; and we ask Him to act in our behalf here and now. Because our faith comes through Jesus, almost every Christian Liturgy has an epiklesis in some form, and it is usually an invocation of the Father to send the Spirit. However, in some anaphoras, the epiklesis is more explicit than in others.

The Byzantine Liturgy has very explicit invocations of the Holy Spirit. St. Basil the Great refers to an epiklesis in his writings on the Holy Spirit: "Have any saints left for us in writing the words to be used in the invocation over the Eucharistic bread and the cup of blessing? As everyone knows, we are not content in the Liturgy simply to recite the words recorded by St. Paul or the Gospels, but we add other words both before and after, words of great importance for this mystery."

The idea that the Spirit comes upon us and empowers us in our worship is very ancient and is still found in the Liturgy today. We saw how, after the great entrance, the deacon and concelebrants say to the presiding priest the words of the angel to Mary, "The Holy Spirit shall come upon you, and the power of the Most High shall overshadow you" (Luke 1:35). The priest responds: "May the Spirit Himself join with us in our celebrations all the days of our lives." In the fourth century St. Cyril of Jerusalem spoke very clearly of the epiklesis: "We beseech the merciful God to send forth His Holy Spirit upon the gifts lying before Him; that He may make the bread the body of Christ, and the wine the blood of Christ, for whatsoever the Holy Spirit has touched, is surely sanctified and changed." By the time of John of Damascus in the eighth century this was the Church's teaching: "For just as God made all that He made by the energy of the Holy Spirit, so also now the energy of the Spirit performs those things that are above nature and which it is not possible to comprehend unless by faith alone. 'How shall this be,' said the holy Virgin, 'seeing I know not a man?' And the archangel Gabriel answered her, 'The Holy Spirit shall come upon you, and the power of the Highest shall overshadow you.' And now you ask, how have the bread become Christ's body and the wine and water Christ's blood? And I say to you, 'The Holy Spirit is present and does these things which surpass reason and thought.'"

The Church's faith is that the bread and wine become the body and blood of Christ in the anaphora. The priest cannot transform the gifts by his own human power. It is done only in the power of God through the Holy Spirit. The priest is able to do nothing without the power of the Holy Spirit. The words of institution are the first sign of the power and gift and revelation of the love of Christ in giving us the Eucharist. The epiklesis is the sign that the priest acts through the gift of the Spirit given through the sacramental mystery of orders. St. John Chrysostom tells us clearly, "The priest does nothing, nor is the right accomplishment of the offered gifts due to human nature; but the grace of the Spirit being present, and coming down on all, makes complete that mystical sacrifice; for even though a man be present, it is God who works through him" (Homily 50 on Pentecost). This is awesome for us mortals. Though in the Divine Liturgy, we cannot see God's action with our physical eyes, we can perceive what is happening in faith.

St. John Chrysostom knew this, and so he described what is mystically happening here, "The priest stands, bringing down not fire, but the Holy Spirit; and he offers prayer at length, not that a fire may be kindled above and destroy the offering [cf. 1 Kings 18:34], but that grace may fall on the sacrifice through that prayer, and kindle the souls of all" (*On the Priesthood* 6,4). This is why he asks that there be an attitude of reverence in the church when the Spirit is invoked, "What are you doing, O man? When the priest stands before the table, stretching forth his hands to heaven, calling on the Holy Spirit to be present, and to touch the oblations, there is a great stillness, a great silence. When the Spirit gives the grace, when He descends, and when He touches the oblations, when you see the Lamb slain and prepared, then do you bring in as well a noise, or disorder, or contentiousness, or railing?" (*De coemet.*

appel. 3)

Hearing the epiklesis aloud teaches us that, even though the priest is saying the words, the power and action of transformation is done by God through His Holy Spirit. The service that we offer to God, then, is really a "Divine" Liturgy, for while we perform the ritual, God the Creator, who has given us the natural ability to pray and implore, is present as our Sanctifier and makes our created offerings a share in His divine life. For this reason, we can never completely express the mystery of the Liturgy.

The Goal of the Anaphora

When the priest prays the epiklesis — and only he can do so through the gift of the grace of the Spirit given him in ordination — he asks God to "send down your Holy Spirit upon us and upon these gifts here set forth" that our reception of these gifts in Communion may be fruitful and saving. Here we see clearly the goal of the anaphora, which is not simply to sanctify bread and wine — though certainly a theological case could be made that this salvation is achieved in union with all creation — but through their transformation, to make us holy children of God and to bring us to the fullness of life through communion in them. Here we stand at the very center of our redemption.

The Anaphora of St. John Chrysostom enumerates five of these desired effects: a spirit of vigilance, the forgiveness of sins; communion (fellowship) in the Holy Spirit; the fullness of the heavenly kingdom; and confidence in God. The central aim of the Liturgy is expressed in the third gift, that of communion. This gift is also mentioned in the Anaphora of St. Basil: "...that all of us who become partakers of this one bread and cup may be united with one another in the communion of the one Holy Spirit..."

The term "Communion" comes from a Greek word (*koinonia*) whose basic meaning is "association," or "connection." In the life of the Church it is applied to our "sharing" or "taking part in" the divine life, the Eucharist, or the Christian community. In Greek, it has many dimensions. Irenaeus already uses it for our union with God: "To as many as continue in their love towards God, does He grant communion with Him, which is life and light, and the enjoyment of all the benefits He has in store..." (*Adv. Haer.* 5, 27, 2). St. Gregory the Theologian expresses the Eucharistic meaning of communion very clearly: "Jesus Himself in an upper chamber gave the communion of the mystery to those who were being initiated into the higher mysteries, that thereby might be shown on the one hand that God must come down to us, ... and on the other that we must go up to Him, and that so there should come to pass a communion of God with human beings" (*On Pentecost*, 41, 12). In the fourth century, it became the word used for the reception of the Eucharist.

Communion may also mean table fellowship or community life, indicating that all the faithful must live with a Christ-like love for one another. The Divine Liturgy is the continuation and concrete expression of the mystery of the incarnation, the Word of God taking human nature, by which God and humanity are united, and by which we also are united together in community, becoming the Body of Christ (Ephesians 1:22-23). St. Gregory of Nyssa tells us that, "human weakness is changed for the better by its communion with the imperishable divine power" (*Contra Eunomium* 6.2).

The first effect sought in the epiklesis is "a spirit of vigilance." The Christian must be "watchful" of his or her soul, and "sober" at all times. This is interesting advice for a culture that emphasizes living life to its fullest, and is prone to addiction, the opposite of sobriety in all its forms. Sobriety and wakefulness are the marks of a Christian: "Let us not be asleep like the rest, but awake and sober... We who live by day must be alert, putting on faith and love as a breastplate and the hope of salvation as a helmet" (1 Thessalonians 5:6-8; cf. 1 Peter 1:13 and 5:8; 2 Timothy 4:5). In other words, spiritual vigilance is a gift of the Holy Spirit, so that the Christian can be well-balanced, self-controlled and self-possessed under all circumstances. This is certainly very difficult in the present age, and probably was pretty difficult in any age, but remains the ideal for the life in Christ.

The second effect of communion in the Eucharist is the forgiveness of sins. This is mentioned when the priest distributes

Communion to each person: "The servant of God (name) receives the precious body and blood of our Lord and God and Savior Jesus Christ, for the forgiveness of sins and for life everlasting." It is a part of the Church teaching, often forgotten, that the Eucharist is the source of the forgiveness of sins. The rite of reconciliation, which is usually called Confession, from the its most evident feature, and which is necessary for the sake of the discipline of the spiritual life of the Church, is a supporting sacramental mystery designed to restore to full communion a person barred from it by reason of grave sin. It makes no sense outside of the Eucharist. This is the traditional teaching of both the Eastern Churches and also of the Roman Catholic Church, as the Council of Trent witnessed, "...appeased by this oblation [the Mass], the Lord, granting the grace and gift of penitence, pardons crimes and even great sins... if contrite and penitent we approach God with a sincere heart and a right faith." Communion, as the reception of the body and blood of Christ, which was broken and shed for the forgiveness of sin, cannot but wipe away all our sins, if we receive this gift of the Spirit worthily and with the right intention. The noted Roman Catholic theologian J-M. Tillard explained:

> "In the most realistic sense of the term, the Eucharist is the sacrament of forgiveness, because it is the sacramental presence and communication of the act which remits sins: as the remembrance of the expiation of the cross, it applies that expiation to those who celebrate the memorial by putting them in touch, through the bread and the cup of the meal, with the 'once and for all' of the paschal event itself, and calls down on the whole world the infinite mercy of God, the Father of Jesus. Within the Church, it is properly speaking the location of redemption" (*The Bread and the Cup of Reconciliation*, 47).

The presence of the Spirit is also invoked to bring about the fullness of the heavenly kingdom through the Eucharist. The fullness of the kingdom here means that the Church might truly fulfill all its potential for salvation in the world in which we live. The word "heavenly" was added later, and it should not mislead us to think that the fullness of the "heavenly" kingdom cannot come until the second coming of our Lord. This may seem to be the case, since our world never seems to be perfect, and, in fact, fails to attain God's will in many ways. We must have confidence, however, that it is possible, and that the more we allow the grace of God to work, the closer we can come to this fullness. In the prayer before the Our Father, which we will discuss later, and which gives a similar list of blessings, we ask for the "inheritance of the heavenly kingdom," here properly in the future.

"Fullness" translates one of the richest Greek theological concepts, the *pleroma*. We find it again in the Liturgy at Communion time, when the priest unites the body of Christ with the cup, saying, "The fullness of the Holy Spirit." In St. Paul's Letter to the Ephesians, it is applied to the Church, as fulfilling all thing in Christ, "And he put all things beneath his feet and gave him as head over all thing to the Church, which is his body, the fullness of the one who fills all things in every way" (Ephesians 1:22). This same idea is found in Colossians 2:9: "In Christ the fullness of deity resides in bodily form. Yours is a share of this fullness, in him who is the head of every principality and power." We are praying, then, that the Church become completely Christ, which is signified by the Eucharist itself, that it become full in numbers, encompassing every human being, and that it become complete in its mission to sanctify the world.

St Athanasius links this gift with John 1:16, "From his fullness we have all received, grace in place of grace." The grace of the Lord Jesus Christ, His gift to us, is the Holy Spirit. Therefore, we "have the grace of the Spirit, receiving it from [Christ's] fullness" (*Oratio contra Arianos* 1.51). In his commentary on the Liturgy, St. Maximos the Confessor says that, "in the [Holy Spirit] are found the fullness of all goodness and the treasures of knowledge and the secrets of wisdom" (*The Church's Mystagogy* 7).

It should become abundantly clear that one who receives communion in the Holy Spirit cannot be a wimp. The Spirit is the wisdom and the power of God. He drives out all sin, purifies the soul and conscience and empowers the mission of the Church to bring about the fullness of all creation. We can no longer live in fear and doubt. The anaphora is the commemoration of the resurrection of the Lord, which filled the apostles with confidence after the fearful days of His passion and burial. The Acts of the Apostles describes the effect this had on the disciples: "And now, Lord, take note of their threats [that is, those opposed to Christ], and enable your servants to speak your word with all boldness, as you stretch forth {your] hand to heal, and signs and wonders are done through the name of your holy servant Jesus" (Acts 4:29). Therefore, the last gift we pray for in the epiklesis is for "boldness," or "confidence." For the Fathers, confidence (Greek, *parresia*) was one of the gifts of Adam in Paradise, and which was lost by sin. With the coming of Christ, this confidence is regained. St. Paul wrote, then, "In Christ and through faith in him we can speak freely to God, drawing near him with confidence" (Ephesians 3:12). This boldness is often identified with "freedom of speech." The Christian is the one who fearlessly proclaims the truth and salvation of Christ.

The gift of confidence is often connected with the Lord's Prayer. In Christ, we can now "make bold" to call God our Father. In the Divine Liturgy the Lord's Prayer is introduced with the words, "And grant, O Lord, that we may with confidence, without condemnation dare call upon You, Father, the God of heaven, and say…" A similar introduction is found in almost all Eucharistic Liturgies.

The epiklesis ends with the words, "and not for judgment or condemnation." This negative petition seems to be in apposition to the final fruit, confidence. St. Basil's epiklesis has the same idea, "…that none of us partake of the holy body and blood of your Christ for judgment or condemnation," and may be founded on St. Paul's warning, "He who eats and drinks without recognizing the body eats and drinks judgment on himself" (1 Corinthians 11:29).

The Anaphora: The Remembrances

After the invocation of the Holy Spirit, the priest remembers the needs of the deceased and living Christians. Prayer of intercession that incorporates the needs of the local community expresses our communion in the Body of Christ.   It is we who need this solidarity, because God knows our needs in advance, as the Liturgy of St. Basil so eloquently points out: "Remember, O Lord our God, all your people... granting those petitions which are for their salvation... because, O God, You know the name and age of all, You know each one even from his mother's womb... You know each one and his requests, each home and its needs." The petitions awaken in us an awareness of our dependency upon God for everything and for the needs of our neighbors.

In both the remembrance of the dead and the living, the presiding priest begins the commemoration.   In the Byzantine Liturgy today the dead are named first. The priest says, "We offer you this spiritual sacrifice for those departed in faith" then remembers the saints by category: 1) forefathers; 2) fathers; 3) patriarchs; 4) prophets; 5) apostles; 6) preachers; 7) evangelists; 8) martyrs; 9) confessors; 10) ascetics; 11) every just spirit.   This commemoration is almost exactly the same in the Anaphoras of St. Basil and John Chrysostom. If you omit the first and last categories ("forefathers," which is a duplication of "fathers," and "all the just") you are left with nine categories of saints, arranged in three groups: 1) fathers, patriarchs, prophets (Old Testament); 2) apostles, preachers, evangelists (New Testament); 3) martyrs, confessors, ascetics (Church). These would then correspond to the nine choirs of angels.

"Especially," he continues, "for our most holy, most pure, most blessed and glorious Lady, the Theotokos and Ever-virgin Mary." Some might find it strange to offer the Liturgy "for" the Mother of God and the saints, but this is not a real problem. The Liturgy, which is our participation in the death and resurrection of the Lord, is accomplished for all people, and Mary is the first and foremost among those people who are saved.   After the Mother of God, then, one particular prophet, John, is named and the apostles are commemorated as a group again.   The priest continues by remembering the Saint commemorated on the day and all saints. Then he may name those he wishes of the departed. Originally the deacon would read the names of the departed written on diptychs ("double writing tablets"). This structure was introduced into the Byzantine Church in the time of the Patriarch Gennadios I (358-371). Today the priest has taken over what diptychs for the dead remain.

The incensing that takes place at this point is not an incensing of the altar, nor is it in honor of the Mother of God. The general rule was that when the dead were commemorated, incense was offered on their behalf. Incense had come to represent our prayer rising to God. "Another angel came and stood at the altar, holding a gold censer. He was given a great quantity of incense to offer, along with the prayers of all the holy ones, on the gold altar that was before the throne. The smoke of the incense along with the prayers of the holy ones went up before God from the hand of the angel" (Revelation 6:3-4).

Today, the intercessions are interrupted by a hymn sung by the faithful in honor of the Mother of God, "It is truly proper to glorify you..." This practice appeared in the tenth century, first before the commemoration of the Virgin, then after it, first silently by the deacon or concelebrating clergy, then aloud by the faithful. The first hymn used was the "Hail, Mary..." Since 1380, the hymn "It is truly proper..." or the irmos of the ninth ode of the matins canon for the feast have been used. "It is truly proper..." and "More honorable..." are actually two separate hymns. "More honorable..." is the irmos of the ninth ode of Good Friday matins. It is based on an ancient hymn of St. Ephrem the Syrian, "More honorable than the Cherubim, and incomparably [so] than all the heavenly armies."

In the same way as for the deceased, the first commemoration of the living for whom we pray was made by a priest who commemorated the hierarch, "In the first place, O Lord, remember our Archbishop (Name)." In the modern Liturgy, we remember ("Among the first..." in our present translation) a group of bishops in descending order: Pope (Patriarch); Archbishop, Bishop. Therefore, this commemoration has become "hierarchical," and follows the structure of Church organization.

After the "first of all" intervention of the presider, then the deacon remembered the other living persons from the diptychs. At the end of his list, the deacon would turn to the faithful and exclaim, "and for those whom each one has in mind, and for all your people." The people would respond, "And for all your people." This last exclamation is sung today as, "And remember all your people."

The intercessions for the living are more elaborate than those for the departed in both anaphoras, especially in the Anaphora of St. Basil. St. John Chrysostom's commemoration is rather simple, remembering basically the religious and civil authorities by group, and, in passing, the whole world, the Church and ascetics. After the remnant of the diptychs for the living, there is a set of three intercessions added from the litanies: 1) "Remember, O Lord, this city..." from the eighth petition of the litany of peace; 2) "Remember, O Lord, those who travel...." from the tenth petition of the litany of peace; 3) "Remember, O Lord, those who bear offerings...." from the final petition of the litany after the Gospel.

In the Anaphora of St. Basil this final intercession is in a more elaborate form: "Remember, O Lord, those who have offered these gifts to you, and those from whom, and through whom and the purpose for which they were offered. Remember, O Lord, the donors and benefactors of your holy churches and those who remember the poor." In both Liturgies, "those who remember the poor" is found only in the intercessions of the anaphora. Indeed, in returning to the world after the Liturgy, we are obliged to support the poor and work for their welfare as a mark of Christian charity.

The Anaphora: The Final "Amen"

The anaphora closes with the doxology, "And grant that, with one voice and one heart, we may glorify and praise your most honored and magnificent name, Father, Son and Holy Spirit, now and ever and forever," to which the people respond "Amen." The whole congregation, therefore, joins in the whole prayer of offering by their seal at the end. The "Amen" is the people's ratification of the prayer, just as the "It is proper and just" is the permission to the presider to proceed. The presbyter, by virtue of ordination, receives the authority to pray in the name of the community, but the whole community joins in the prayer with their "Amen."

St. Justin Martyr describes the importance of this "Amen." "There is then brought to the president of the brethren bread and a cup of wine mixed with water; and he, taking them, gives praise and glory to the Father of the universe, through the name of the Son and of the Holy Spirit, and offers thanks at considerable length for our being counted worthy to receive these things at His hands. And when he has concluded the prayers and thanksgivings all the people present express their assent by saying Amen" (First Apology 1, 65.). To say "Amen" was a privilege of being Christian. Dionysius of Alexandria said that he dared not re-baptize "one who had heard the giving of thanks and joined in repeating the Amen" (Eusebius, *Church History* 7,9). St. Cyril of Jerusalem calls the Amen the "seal of the prayer" (*Mystagogical Catechesis* 5) while Jerome mentions that in Rome "the people resounded" with their "Amen" "like heavenly thunder."

"Amen" was obviously a special acclamation in the early Christian community, because it was left in Hebrew and became a ritual word. It means, "Would that it might be so," or more simply, "So be it." The different ordained orders and laity had various functions in the Liturgy, but it is the corporate celebration of one community. Dom Gregory Dix wrote, "The primitive ideal of corporate worship was not the assimilation of the office of the 'order' of laity to those of the other orders, but the combination of all the radically distinct 'liturgies,' of all the orders in a single complete action of the organic Body of Christ" (*The Shape of the Liturgy*, 129). Everyone who takes part in the Liturgy, including the priest, must know their place and role and do it well, so that we can offer as worthy as possible worship to God according to the abilities of our human nature and in co-operation with divine grace.

From this, we see how important it is, when the Liturgy is celebrated in the vernacular, for the priest to read aloud the whole anaphora. This is the more authentic tradition of the Church, and it is reflected in the written rubrics (rules for celebration) that have governed the Liturgy through the centuries. It seems that the prayers only came to be recited softly (*sotto voce*) when the language changed and the people could no longer comprehend the original words. The hymns sung by the people during the anaphora give some insight into its meaning, but, as Theodore of Andidum said in his commentary, it is like trying to identify a cloth by only touching the fringes. The heart of the prayer said by the priest in the name of all the people is the proclamation of the sacrificial and commemorative nature of the Liturgy. In giving us the Eucharist, our Lord said, "Do this in memory of me." We cannot completely fulfill that command unless we do call to mind what God has said and done for us, as is recounted in the anaphora. The public recitation of the anaphora makes us aware of what we believe and what we profess with our hearts and lips and what we accept "with one voice and heart" by saying "Amen — So be it."

For Your Reflection

1. Before the great entrance we are called to "set aside all earthly cares." What do you understand this phrase to mean and how can you follow its direction?

2. How do you think the Divine Liturgy is a "sacrifice of praise"?

3. What are the main "movements" or aspects of the anaphora?

Chapter Four — Communion Rites

At the start of the Divine Liturgy, the deacon invites the priest to begin by saying, "It is time for the Lord to act." First God speaks to us by His word in Holy Scripture and so we hear His voice. The Gospel then comes alive for us, when He comes into our midst at the prayer of the priest and the bread and wine become the body and blood of our Lord and God and Savior Jesus by the power of the Holy Spirit. After the anaphora, God then comes into our very being when we receive His body and blood in Holy Communion as food for our souls and bodies.

Between the anaphora and Holy Communion there is now a rite of preparation for the completion and fulfillment of the Divine Liturgy in which God deifies and sanctifies us. In the apostolic era of our faith, the Liturgy proceeded directly from the prayer of offering (the anaphora) to Communion. However, very soon, this moment in the Liturgy began to fill out. Between the blessing of the gifts and their distribution, rites of preparation for Communion have developed. This preparation involves both the people who shall receive Communion, and the gifts themselves. The peoples' preparation is the recitation of the several prayers proposing different aspects of readiness. The preparation of the gifts includes the ritual breaking of the sacramental body of our Lord, an essential part of the shape of the Liturgy, which has developed from Jewish meal practices. The preparation of the people precedes the preparation of the gifts as a natural outflow of the epiklesis, where the Spirit is invoked, first on the people, then on the gifts. The epiklesis, though, should not be thought of as two separate invocations — it is one, that the Spirit transform us *through* Communion in the body and blood of Christ.

The Litany and First Prayer of Preparation

The first prayer of preparation is said by the priest to conclude the litany that begins, "Let us complete our prayer to the Lord." The text of this prayer is different in the Liturgies of St. John Chrysostom, St. Basil the Great and the Liturgy of the Presanctified Gifts. The prayer that we are most familiar with, from the Liturgy of St. John Chrysostom, basically echoes the text of the epiklesis on the gifts. Instead of asking God to send His Spirit to transform the gifts, making them the body and blood of His Son, here we ask Him "...to make us worthy to partake with a clear conscience of your heavenly and awesome mysteries." Again we see very clearly that the Spirit is the power of God working in our whole lives, transforming the gifts and through them, transforming us to become His worthy children.

In the corresponding prayer at the Liturgy of St. Basil, we ask God to "cleanse us of all defilement of flesh and spirit," and "teach us to attain holiness in fear of you," that we might receive Communion "united to the Body and Blood of your Christ," with a pure witness of our conscience. We pray that we may remain in Communion until the end of our lives and that it may carry us past judgment to those things "prepared for those who love him" (1 Cor 2:9). The sharing we have of Christ here is Christ dwelling in us, and it is only through the mercy and grace of Christ that we can be justified and can reach our end: perfect union with Christ in the new heaven and the new earth.

The parallel prayer in the Liturgy of the Presanctified Gifts is actually the principal prayer in this rite. It serves in place of an anaphora as an anamnesis of the mystery being celebrated and as an explanation of the presanctified gifts.

The Lord's Prayer

The communicants' second prayer of preparation is the Lord's Prayer ("Our Father"), in the universal tradition of all Churches. The Lord's Prayer has always had a unique place in the Church's worship, since the Gospels present it as the words of prayer taught by the Son of God Himself. It is entirely proper that we prepare ourselves for union with Christ by calling God, "our Father," as He taught us, for God is His Father by nature and becomes our Father by adoption, as we are joined physically and spiritually with Jesus.

The Lord's Prayer very early acquired a connection with being initiated into the Christian community, becoming "sons of the living God." Theodoret was to write, "We teach this prayer to none of the uninitiated, only to the faithful. No uninitiated person would dare say, 'Our Father who art in heaven...' before receiving the grace of adoption" (*Compendium of the Falsehood of Heresies* 5). For the apostolic Christians, the most awesome feature of this prayer would have been the ability to call God, "Father," indeed, not only "Father," but *abba*, an Aramaic term of familiarity.

The "Our Father" is also the one liturgical prayer said by the celebrant and the congregation together. Usually, the people just join themselves to liturgical prayers by saying "Amen." Because Jesus taught this prayer to all His followers, all the faithful have the privilege of reciting this prayer. Therefore, the priest introduces this prayer by saying that we can call God, "Father" with confidence.

It would seem that the main reason for placing the Lord's Prayer in the Liturgy before Communion is because of its petition, "give us this day our daily bread." However, what we find is that the liturgical focus, counter to expectation, is on the forgiveness of sins. St. John Chrysostom says, "For whoever called God Father, by this one naming has confessed the forgiveness of sins, the repeal of punishment, justice, sanctification, redemption, the adoption of sons, the inheritance, brotherhood with the only Son and the gift of the Spirit" (*Homily on Matthew* 19, 4).

Since the Liturgy is offered "for the forgiveness of sins," it is natural that a penitential attitude would show itself in preparation for it. We feel ourselves to be sinners and ask forgiveness before receiving such an awesome mystery. I am not using the word "penitential" in our common modern understanding, which has acquired the sense of a kind of punishment for wrongdoing, but in the sense of the change of heart needed to receive Communion fruitfully.   We beg Christ for forgiveness, we wish to die to our sins, we want to live in the communion of the Holy Spirit. Repentance has a positive meaning — it is the conscious choosing of freedom from sin.

We Bow Our Heads to the Lord

The third element in the preparation of the people for Communion is the "prayer at the bowing of heads."   After the Lord's Prayer is sung, the priest again greets the people, "Peace be to all."   Then the deacon commands, "Bow your heads to the Lord."   We then bow our heads in humility while the priest says a prayer for those whose heads are bowed.   There are three different prayers for this moment: one at the Liturgy of St. John Chrysostom, one at the Liturgy of St. Basil and a third for the Liturgy of the Presanctified Gifts.   If I may be permitted a point of liturgical trivia, the prayer at the bowing of heads in the Liturgy of St. Basil is the only one that is shorter than the corresponding prayer in the Liturgy of St. John Chrysostom.

In the past, there have been different attitudes towards the reception of Holy Communion.   To be able to receive the consecrated body and blood of our Lord has always been perceived as a gift of which we are unworthy.   We are able to receive only because God has made us capable of approaching this heavenly banquet.   In early Christianity, in the first days of faith, people accepted the gift of Holy Communion because of the invitation — indeed, the command — of our Lord to partake, "Drink from [this cup], all of you, for this is my blood of the covenant" (Matthew 26:27-28).   To refuse this body and blood would be to refuse union with God, and would leave us outside of salvation.   Indeed, in the Gospel of St. John, Jesus preaches, "Amen, amen, I say to you, unless you eat the flesh of the Son of Man and drink his blood, you do not have life within you" (John 6:53).   To partake of Holy Communion is to manifest our faith in and our solidarity with Christ, who died and rose for the sake of our life, and with his body, the Church (see Ephesians 1:26-27).

After the third century, when the persecution of the Church ceased with Constantine's Edict of Toleration, people began to enter the Church in large numbers. The Fathers saw, as a result of this, a weakening of the fervor of faith. To strengthen that faith, they emphasized the awesomeness of the gift we receive in Communion. The result was that many stopped going to Communion frequently, because they began to perceive themselves as unworthy. Various fasting laws were introduced and some felt that it was necessary to go to confession before Communion, though this was never made a formal Church law. In our time, these practices have been relaxed, because the Church wants to stress the deep spiritual meaning of our Lord's invitation: that He wants us to be saved, to be united with Him, to be godly, that He wants sin to be overcome, eternal life to be attained, and the Kingdom to be established. We cannot do this by our own powers, but only by divine grace.

Besides rigorous standards for preparing to receive Holy Communion, there was also an attitude of penance that accompanied the act of receiving Communion itself. In the Western Church, the faithful were expected to receive Communion on their knees. This practice did not enter the Eastern Church, except in some of the Eastern Catholic Churches that imitated the styles of the West. However, it was not the most authentic theology since, in Communion, we are united with the risen Lord, who lifts us up to life. Certainly, this is not meant as any reflection on the good faith of those who, in the past, knelt for Communion; but it is the more general tradition of both the Western and Eastern Churches to stand to receive.

All of this tells us one truth, that we must approach the holy mysteries of the body and blood of our Lord with an awareness of our unworthiness to receive this divine gift. We likewise symbolize this "awareness of unworthiness" with a public sign given during the Liturgy before we come to Communion. This need for a spirit of humility and repentance is served very appropriately by the act of bowing our heads before the priest elevates the holy Body of our Lord that is to be given to all.

The prayer for those whose heads are bowed in the Liturgy of St. Basil is directly an act of preparation for Holy Communion. The priest prays out of an awareness of our unworthiness, "Make [those who have bowed their heads] worthy to partake of these, your most pure and life-creating mysteries without condemnation for the remission of their sins and for communion of the Holy Spirit." The grace of God making us worthy should manifest itself in the way we live, and so the priest prays, "Turn them away from every evil deed, equip them for every good work." The prayer at the bowing of heads in the Liturgy of the Presanctified Gifts also clearly speaks of Communion: "Make us worthy to partake without condemnation of these your life-creating mysteries, for we have bowed our heads to you expecting your abundant mercy."

The corresponding prayer at the Liturgy of St. John Chrysostom, on the other hand, does not refer to Communion and looks forward more to our return to life in the world after the Liturgy, "O Master, make smooth for the good of all the path that lies ahead." These words, "make smooth the path that lies ahead," have been a problem for translators. Some have tried to add a reference to the holy gifts, but this leads to a strange phrase, "smooth out the gifts before us." It is possible that this prayer had a different function in the Liturgy than to prepare for Communion. We must remember, as mentioned above, that frequent Communion became very rare for a time in the life of the Church. Perhaps this prayer was used as a dismissal prayer for those who were not going to receive Communion. This is very likely when we consider that both the evening office of vespers and the morning service of matins end with a prayer at the bowing of heads as a blessing for our return to life in the world. Even if this is so, the prayer at the bowing of heads in the Liturgy of St. John Chrysostom is now a preparation for Communion, and it is in a spirit of great humility that we approach our God by saying, "Look down from heaven, O Master, upon those who bow their heads to you, for they do not bow to flesh and blood, but to you, the awesome God." We do this likewise in a spirit of thanksgiving to the God who created us out of "nonexistence" and who now makes us worthy to be united with Him for our sanctification.

Holy Gifts to Holy People

When we have prepared by prayer as well as we humanly can for the reception of Communion, the priest then invites us to receive with the words, "Holy gifts to holy people." The original Greek here is much simpler, reading simply *ta aghia tis aghiis* ("The holy to the holy"), which means, "What is holy to those who are holy." I find it always interesting that the more ancient a liturgical text is, the more succinct and dense it is. Only later do we have a passion to get very elaborate. It is also interesting that, while the deacon does most of the liturgical directions and invitations, here it is the priest that issues this first invitation to the assembly, indicating that this phrase is very ancient, going back to a time when the roles in ritual were not yet so clearly delineated.

With this phrase, then, we enter into the mystery of the "holy." We have affirmed this many times during the Liturgy. We sang that God is "holy, ... holy and mighty, ...holy and immortal." In the anaphora, we professed that God is three times holy by singing the hymn of victory: "holy, holy, holy..." Our faith in the holiness of God means that we are aware that He is entirely other than us. The author of *The Divine Names* wrote that God is "mind beyond minds, word beyond speech... as no other being is." God is the "cause of all existence, and therefore transcending existence. ... We must not dare to apply words or conceptions to this hidden transcendent God. We can use only what Scripture has disclosed" (1,1-2). God revealed Himself to Moses by saying, "My face you cannot see, for no man sees me and still lives" (Exodus 33:20). It is impossible for us to approach God in any way, to understand Him with our finite minds, to be worthy of Him by any merit or effort of our own. Yet this same God has come and dwelt among us, and in Jesus our Lord He revealed Himself to us and has let us see His face, "the refulgence of his glory, the very imprint of his being" (Hebrews 1:3). Yet at every Communion, we are invited into the presence of the holy, and to partake of the very body and blood of our Lord Himself. This is so only because of the incomprehensible mercy and love of God for us, His beloved creatures. We can approach God only because He has come to us. This is ultimately what every Liturgy is about.

What are the "holy gifts?" The original Greek only says "holy things," but this very clearly refers to the gifts of bread and wine that we have offered, and that the Holy Spirit has made to be the body and blood of our Lord Jesus Christ, now given by God as a gift to us. Who are the "holy people?" Again, the Greek says only, "those who are holy," but again refers clearly to those about to receive the gifts of Christ's body and blood. Can we conclude from this that only those who are saints may receive Communion, and that most of us are unworthy? St. Paul warns, "Whoever eats the bread or drinks the cup unworthily sins against the body and blood of the Lord" (1 Cor 11:27). Indeed, we should receive Holy Communion with a sense of unworthiness, and with a spirit of wonder and reverence that God would consider us worthy of so great a gift. However, we must not allow ourselves to refuse the gift, for this would be weakness, a failure to enter into the relationship with God that He has commanded of us and invited us to in His infinite wisdom and love. Therefore, the second invitation to Communion, issued by the deacon, is in the form of a command, "Approach..." and he adds "with the fear of God and with faith." We must come forward with great reverence but if we do not accept the invitation, we do not have the commitment of faith needed for salvation. That is why Jesus teaches us, "Unless you eat the flesh of the Son of Man and drink his blood, you do not have life within you" (John 6:53).

The phrase "for the holy," must have some meaning, though. It cannot mean that everyone can receive Communion. Some may come forward but others may not. An early non-canonical work gives the most probable explanation, "But let no one eat or drink from your Eucharist except those who are baptized in the Lord's name, for the Lord also has spoken concerning this: 'Do not give what is holy to dogs [Matthew 7:6]'" (*Didache* 9,5). This seems to be a way of referring to baptism. To approach the Eucharist "unworthily" here means to receive without baptism. The authentic response to this unworthiness, then, would not be to reject Communion, but to receive baptism, if we have not done so yet. This is also an indication that in the very early Church, the non-baptized were permitted to be present at the Eucharist, but could not receive. It is also true for the baptized that certain great sins make us "unworthy" of Communion, because they have stained our baptisms, destroying our life in Christ. To remedy this, we must first accept the rite of confession and repentance, which the Fathers called "the second baptism." Therefore, it is the baptized members of the Church whom St. Paul often refers to as "saints," "holy ones." Nicholas Cabasilas explains, "Those whom the priest calls holy are not only those who have attained perfection, but those also who are striving for it without having yet obtained it. ... It is in this sense that the whole Church is called holy, and that the Apostle, writing to the Christian people as a whole, says to them, 'Holy brethren, partakers of the heavenly calling' [Heb 3:1]" (*Commentary on the Divine Liturgy*, 36:1-5).

Our response to this invitation is the hymn, "One is holy, one is Lord, Jesus Christ, to the glory of God the Father." This is a popular acclamation, taken from the Great Doxology, which may be translated literally, "One holy! One Lord, Jesus Christ!" Such acclamations were popular in ancient times. The holy things were the body and blood of Christ, so it is natural that the faithful would shout out that only Christ was holy. The response itself is like a commentary on 1 Corinthians 8:6, "For although there may be so-called gods in heaven, or on earth... yet for us there is one God, the Father, from whom are all things, and for whom we exist, and one Lord Jesus Christ, through whom are all things and through whom we exist." Again, the best commentary on the hymn is by Nicholas Cabasilas: "When the priest says: 'Holy things to the holy,' the faithful reply: 'One is holy, one is Lord, Jesus Christ, in the glory of God the Father.' For no one has holiness of himself; it is not the consequence of human virtue, but comes to all from Him and through Him. It is as if we were to place mirrors beneath the sun; each would shine, and send forth rays of light, so that one would think there were many suns; yet in truth there is but one sun which shines in all; just so Christ, the only Holy One, pours Himself forth upon the faithful, shines in so many souls, and gives light to many saints; yet He alone is holy, in the glory of the Father" (*Commentary* 36, 5).

The Preparation of the Chalice

When the priest invites the faithful to receive Holy Communion, he takes the bread that has been consecrated to become the body of our Lord, and lifts it from the diskos saying, "Holy gifts for holy people;" that is, the body and blood of our Lord that has been offered is for those who have been sanctified in baptism. This begins the preparation of the consecrated gifts for distribution to the people. This very first time that he touches the body of our Lord itself is an act of revelation, as the priest stands in the place of the holy prophet John the Baptizer, who pointed Jesus out to the crowds, "Behold the Lamb of God who takes away the sin of the world" (John 1:29).

The consecrated central portion of the bread is called "the Lamb" (*amnos* in Greek, *ahnec* in Slavonic). Jesus as the Lamb of God recalls the prophecy of Isaiah about the sufferings of the Messiah: "Like a lamb led to slaughter or a sheep before the shearers, he was silent and opened not his mouth... he was... smitten for the sins of his people" (Isaiah 53:7-8). This identification of the bread was already indicated in the Rite of Preparation for the Divine Liturgy. Now, after the anaphora and before the Communion, the prophecy, as it were, is fulfilled. The Divine Liturgy, we have seen, is a representation of Christ's sacrifice. Our Lord, the completely innocent Lamb of God, took upon Himself the consequences of our sin, and offered His life as an act of obedience to the Father. We see this in Christ's prayer in the garden before He is arrested, "Not my will but yours be done" (Luke 22:42). By doing this, our Lord erased our sins, and gave us access to eternal life. We enter into this mystery at each Divine Liturgy, which is identified mystically — in an unbloody way — with our Lord's sacrifice.

We see the same mystery foretold in the story of Abraham's sacrifice of his son Isaac (Genesis 22). In obedience to God, Abraham is willing to return his only son, given to him wondrously by God, in sacrifice to God. God, however, refuses this offering and reveals a ram to him, which Abraham then kills in sacrifice. Jesus replaces that ram, and the Father completes that which He did not require from Abraham so that the people He created and loves might be freed from sin and have life everlasting. This happens mystically in every Divine Liturgy. We receive Communion from this Lamb, who offered Himself out of love and is therefore glorified in His love and becomes life-giving, "Worthy is the Lamb that was slain to receive power and riches, wisdom and strength, honor and glory and blessing ... for you were slain and with your blood you purchased for God those from every tribe and tongue, people and nation" (Revelation 5:12.9). This is the gift God gives us in Communion.

The priest then takes the Lamb and breaks it into four pieces. This action is known as the "fraction," (nothing mathematical, but from the Latin word *fractio*, meaning "a breaking"). The breaking of the bread goes back to the original roots of our faith, for it was a Jewish practice to "break bread" and distribute it to the family gathered at table as a sign of their unity. This is exactly how St. Paul understands it in the inspired Scripture, "The bread that we break, is it not a participation in the body of Christ? Because the loaf of bread is one, we, though many, are one body, for we all partake of the one loaf" (1 Corinthians 10:16-17). This is why the breaking of the bread is an essential part of the Divine Liturgy and to omit it is to empty the Liturgy of its essential meaning, that we are one in Christ and in Christ united with one another. This is what Christ prays for at the Last Supper, "that they may all be one, as you, Father, are in me and I in you, that they also may be one in us" (John 17:21). The fraction is an act of union, for while the bread is broken apart for distribution in Communion, Christ is never divided and brings together all who partake of a portion of the bread which has become His body. Therefore, the priest says as he breaks the Lamb, "Broken and distributed is the Lamb of

God, broken yet never divided, ever eaten yet never consumed, but sanctifying those who partake thereof," for Christ is totally present in each Eucharistic particle.

The consecrated bread is first divided into four portions and arranged on the diskos (plate) in the form of a cross. Since Communion is for the baptized, this symbolizes our baptism, as St. Paul explains, "we who were baptized into Christ Jesus were baptized into his death" (Romans 6:3). Up to this point in the Liturgy, the bread that is the body of Christ has been on the diskos, to the left of the cup of wine that is the blood of Christ. This separation of bread and wine is an image of the death of our Lord, for when the soldier pierced the side of Christ on the cross, "immediately blood and water flowed out" (John 19:34). This is one reason why the chalice always contains a mixture of wine and water. However, now the priest takes one part of the Lamb and unites it with the blood in the cup saying, "The fullness of the Holy Spirit." This union (in Greek, *henosis*) of the bread and the cup is therefore the full revelation of the presence of the Risen Christ. In Communion we do not receive a dead body, but the risen Christ, who takes away sin and gives us everlasting life.

The chalice is then further prepared by the pouring of the *zeon*, or hot water. The original purpose of this rite is not clear, but it certainly was not to melt wine that may have frozen in churches in cold climes. It now has a symbolic function, to represent the fervor of our faith that the Holy Spirit pours into our hearts as we receive Holy Communion. When the hot water is poured, the deacon or priest says, "The fervor of faith, full of the Holy Spirit." This practice was dropped by our Church at the Synod of Zamosc in 1720, out of fear of adding too much water to the chalice. It was restored in the Divine Liturgy prescribed by Rome in 1941, but only at the discretion of the bishop. The rite of zeon has now been mandated by the Liturgical Instruction of January 6, 1996, paragraph 67.

One task remains before the distribution of Holy Communion. In accordance with St. Paul's principle mentioned above, "we, though many, are one body, for we all partake of the one loaf" (1

Corinthians 10:17), the priest then divides the reminder of the Lamb, the "one loaf" into as many particles as needed for Communion. This division is called the "comminution." This practice is scrupulously observed in most Byzantine Churches, because of its Scriptural origin, but in the eighteenth century, to imitate the Roman practice of using individual hosts, the bread to be used in Communion began to be cut into particles before the celebration of the Divine Liturgy. In any case, renewed care that the Communion distributed at the Liturgy be taken from one loaf is a witness to the unity between God and us, and us with one another, that is the goal of the Liturgy.

The Climax of Everything

When it is time for Holy Communion, the deacon invites us to receive with the words, "Approach with the fear of God and with faith." Without faith, we do not see or receive the mystery, but in faith we are one in Christ. Some liturgical traditions also add, "and with love," because many today see "fear" as a negative virtue. "Fear" here, though, also means love, because we must approach Communion in the body and blood of our Lord with a sense of wonder for God's love for us.

In his commentary on the Divine Liturgy, St. Maximos the Confessor describes Holy Communion as "...the climax of everything... which transforms into itself and renders similar to the causal good (that is, God) by grace and participation those who worthily share in it. To them is there lacking nothing of this good that is possible and attainable for human beings, so that they also can be and be called gods by adoption through grace because all of God entirely fills them and leaves no part of them empty of his presence" (*The Church's Mystagogy*, chapter 21). Here St. Maximos expresses beautifully the theology of our faith: God created us in His own image, and in partaking of the body and blood of Christ, we are restored and fulfilled with that image, and are made Godlike, becoming what we have eaten. This is the covenant of Jesus, the Son and Word of God, given to us on the evening of His arrest and sealed by His death on the cross and by

His holy resurrection.   Therefore, when the priest gives Holy
Communion, he says, "The servant of God (*name*) partakes of the
precious, most holy, and most pure body and blood of our Lord,
God and Savior, Jesus Christ for the remission of (his *or* her) sins
and for life everlasting.   Amen." (The new translation eliminates
the distinction between "servants" and "handmaids.")

This is the climax of the Liturgy, the completion of the
sacrifice, our deification, the gift of the fruit of the Tree of Life, the
attainment of our human destiny to transcend our mortal
limitations, the promise of our future inheritance, the seal of the
Divine Liturgy, of the love of God for us manifested through His
death and resurrection.   It is a gift of God, and must be received
with great joy.   By Communion, God raises us up from our
unworthiness and therefore we receive Communion standing.   It is
a sign of our faith that God saves us through this grace.   What St.
John Chrysostom wrote about mystery is fulfilled in the Holy
Communion of the Eucharist.   We see one thing with the eyes of
our body, but another with the eyes of our soul.   With the eyes of
our body we see only bread and wine, and receive with our tongues
only a small portion of this bread and wine, but with spiritual eyes
we see the "noetic" — that is, the deeper and more real — truth:
that we are partaking of the body and blood of our Lord, the
incarnate Word of God.   In this way we are brought into unity with
the Creator of all, both what is visible and what is invisible, as
expressed so well in the prayer of thanksgiving at St. Basil's
Liturgy, "a faith that cannot be confounded, a love that does not
pretend, a wisdom that overflows, the healing of our souls and
bodies, the defeat of every enemy [that is, spiritual enemies of our
soul], the full observance of your commandments, and an
acceptable defense before the fearsome judgment seat of your
Christ."

In the ancient Church, closer to the apostolic norms, it was
expected that every person who attended the Liturgy would receive
Holy Communion.   It was not an option, it was the reason anyone
was there, and to partake was an act of faith that we are the Body of
Christ, that Christ has invited us to unity in the Trinity, that the

only fulfillment of our human destiny to be an image of God. Those who were unable to receive Holy Communion were dismissed from the church before the anaphora, the prayer of offering, was said, for having heard the prayer, we could only assent in faith and receive the gift. This tradition has been maintained to this day for those who are ordained bishop, priest or deacon and who serve at the holy table. They cannot abstain from Communion and must receive. This was also true for all the faithful, and those who were not yet baptized, the catechumens, were dismissed before bread and wine were brought to the holy table. Likewise, those who had committed grave sins that made them unworthy of their baptism, and were under church penance were likewise dismissed at the same time. As we have seen, there are indications that those who were not going to receive Communion at the Liturgy were also dismissed by a prayer at the bowing of heads, which may remain in the Liturgy before Communion. However, as the ancient fervor diminished, and the teachers of the Church emphasized the awesomeness of the mystery, many others began to spontaneously abstain from partaking in Communion, even when they were present for the whole Liturgy. The situation persisted for many centuries that the faithful would receive the Eucharist only once or twice a year. A more proper attitude towards Communion has been restored over the last century, but modern individualism still makes our participation in Communion a matter of personal preference, a matter of our private share of God's grace rather than incorporation into the salvation of the people of God, the Church.

Holy Communion brings us into a real unity. Through the body and blood of our Lord Jesus Christ, we are united in both body and spirit with the Son of God, and through Him, we become partakers in the life of the Trinity. Through Him, we also are united with the whole Church, which, St. Paul tells us, is the Body of Christ (Ephesians 1:22-23). We must question whether our faith in this reality is strong or weak. If it is strong, then the reception of Communion is the most important act we do as Christians. If it is unity with God and His Church, then we must celebrate it as a sign of unity. This is why St. Paul again emphasizes that we should partake of one loaf (1 Corinthians 10:17). This is why St. John Chrysostom so often taught that in the Eucharist we are all equal, for all of us, becoming one in Christ, are one body and no one is superior to another. We are all transformed into Christ, who is infinitely greater than any of us, and all of us together.

To serve this unity, Communion should be received by all as a corporate body, for we are all servants of God. Communion should be given at one time to all present in the church, the priest first as the elder of the community, though, as Chrysostom tells us, he receives no special benefit this way, since we are all one and equal in Christ. The only exception is for those who are ill and unable to come to church. The Eucharist is taken to them outside the Liturgy. Likewise, Communion should not be delayed until after the Divine Liturgy, as has become the custom for singers in some places, so as not to interrupt the liturgical chant. However, it is better to have a moment of silence for the sake of the unity of the whole community.

We Give You Thanks

St. Maximos the Confessor said that Holy Communion was "the climax of everything," so that one could say, I suppose, that the rest of the Divine Liturgy is "anti-climatic." In fact, the Church does close the Liturgy rather quickly after Holy Communion has been received by the faithful. However, two important prayers remain to be said, one in thanksgiving for the gift we have received and the other as a summary and conclusion of the whole Liturgy. There is also the ancient hymn, "May our mouth be filled with your praise..." In the Liturgy of the Presanctified Gifts, this hymn is replaced by another that I quote simply because it sums up so clearly what this part of the Liturgy is about. "We give you thanks, O Christ our God, that you have made us sharers of the mystery of your redemption, your pure body and precious blood, poured forth for the world unto the forgiveness of sins." Father Robert Taft has shown that this is actually a prayer from the Syrian Church that the Ruthenian Church has adapted as a hymn.

The blessings received in Holy Communion, as we have seen, are beyond the comprehension of human understanding. It is, therefore, entirely appropriate that we express our thanksgiving for this gift. There are three prayers that are of primary importance in the Liturgy. The first is the prayer after the great entrance, in which we ask God to enable us to offer the sacrifice of the Divine Liturgy, since it is, after all, the divine offering of God's only Son. The second is the prayer of offering itself, the anaphora. The third is the prayer of thanksgiving after we have received Communion. One might question that if the anaphora itself might also be called "Eucharist," a prayer of thanksgiving, then why would this prayer be necessary. The anaphora of the Liturgy is the great prayer of thanksgiving for all the wondrous deeds God has done on our behalf. In this prayer, the Lord acts again, making the bread and wine His body and blood, making His salvation real here and now, so that, through our partaking of this divinely bestowed food, we are truly sanctified.

The prayer of thanksgiving after Communion is specifically offered because God has allowed us to take part in this mystery of redemption. We see this in the text of the prayers themselves. We thank you "...that this day you have made us worthy of your heavenly and immortal mysteries" (Liturgy of St. John Chrysostom) and "...for our sharing in your holy, most pure, immortal and heavenly mysteries, which you have given us for the benefit, sanctification, and healing of our souls and bodies" (Liturgy of St. Basil).

Note carefully the complete change of tone from previous prayers. Before our Communion, we implored God to make us worthy, now we thank Him that He has made us worthy. In fact, if we have received our Lord's body and blood with a sincere heart, the Spirit would not allow sin to remain in us and we are cleansed of our unworthiness. This is also proclaimed in the hymn we sing to conclude Holy Communion, "You have deemed us worthy to partake of Your holy, divine, immortal, pure and life-creating mysteries." We have been sanctified, and so we ask God, "keep us in Your holiness." This is the same as asking to be kept in Christ whom we have received, and "who became for us wisdom from God, as well as righteousness, sanctification and redemption" (1 Corinthians 1:30). The introduction of this hymn can be traced to the year 624, when it was placed in the Liturgy by the Patriarch Sergius. It opens with a quotation from Psalm 70, "May our mouth be filled with Your praise, O Lord, so that we may sing of Your glory" (v. 8).

Between Holy Communion and this formal thanksgiving that God has deemed us worthy of receiving, a blessing with the Holy Eucharist is inserted. This blessing is taken from Psalm 26, "Save your people, O God, and bless your inheritance." We respond to this by singing a hymn from the office of Pentecost Sunday, "We have seen the true light, we have received the heavenly Spirit." This blessing was added much more recently than the prayer of thanksgiving. It was not added to the Presanctified Liturgy, and the hymn itself is frequently changed. From Pascha to Pentecost we sing the Paschal troparion, "Christ is risen from the dead..." and during the Feast of the Ascension of our Lord, we sing the verse, "Be exalted above the heavens, O God, and let your glory be over all the earth." (Psalm 56:5). This psalm verse tells us that the risen Jesus we receive is glorified at the right hand of the Father, "Christ in you, the hope for glory" (Colossians 1:27). This passage from the psalms is also repeated by the priest as he censes the holy gifts before taking them from the holy table to the table of preparation to be consumed.

The resurrection of Christ was a manifestation of God's power, and since the Trinity is one God, Jesus rose with the power of the Spirit. His first action after the resurrection was to breathe upon the apostles in the upper room with the words, "Receive the Holy Spirit" (John 20:22) and on the fiftieth day sent the Holy Spirit upon the believers gathered in the upper room. And so the hymn "We have seen the true light..." is a profession of faith that we have received the risen Lord, who gives us life through the gift of the Holy Spirit.

Communion brings about a real transformation, like in the first disciples, who were transformed from fearful fishermen to zealous witnesses to the Gospel of His resurrection. This is why faith is such an important component of Holy Communion, for if we are open to God's grace, "all of us... are being transformed into the same image from glory to glory, as from the Lord who is the Spirit" (2 Corinthians 3:18). The possibilities of Holy Communion are infinite.

The Ambon Prayer

As the Divine Liturgy draws to a close, the priest proclaims words that remind us of Jesus' words to His followers after the resurrection, "Peace be to you." He invites the assembly, "Let us go forth in peace," and the people respond, "in the name of the Lord." The priest then concludes with a prayer that summarizes the mystery of Holy Communion: "Preserve the fullness of your Church, sanctify those who love the beauty of your house, glorify them in return by your divine power... for every perfect gift is from above, coming down from you, the Father of lights" (James 1:17).

We popularly call this the "Ambon Prayer," and for this reason it is sometimes said on the small circular extension from the altar platform called the solea, where the Gospel is generally read today. The ambon was originally a raised platform in the middle of the nave, the main body of the Church, connected to the sanctuary by a walkway. Readers proclaimed the Scriptures from this structure that they might be clearly heard. At one time this prayer was read by the priest as he passed the ambon in procession from the church and is therefore called "the prayer *behind* the ambon." Today, the rubrics (directions) for the Divine Liturgy prescribe that this prayer be said in the middle of the nave.

There were at one time many different ambon prayers to express the different mysteries of the Church's year of grace. In general, these ambon prayers see the multiplicity of God's works in our behalf through the lens of Holy Communion in the risen Lord. God lives in us in all that He has accomplished and in all the circumstances of our life, so that, as we leave the Divine Liturgy, we can say with St. Paul, "yet I live, no longer I, but Christ lives in me" (Galatians 2:20).

There were originally no further prayers or blessings at the Divine Liturgy, for what greater blessing is there than to have received the body and blood of Christ. The priest's invocation, "The blessing of our Lord be upon you..." which now follows the ambon prayer was for the distribution of antidoron, actually a complement to the Eucharist. The dismissal is a prayer that Christ may "have mercy on us and save us," as we return into the world which is not yet perfectly saved, and which, as St. Paul tells us, "is groaning in labor pains even until now." (Romans 8: 22)

Consuming the Holy Gifts

In the Byzantine tradition, we do not immediately consume the holy body and precious blood that is left after Communion. As we have seen, we first carry what remains back to the table of preparation as an image of the ascension. Then, when the final prayer of the Liturgy has been offered, the deacon (or priest) reverently eats and drinks the remaining holy gifts and cleanses the chalice. The priest says a private prayer for this act of consummation, which expresses both the reality of what has happened by God's power, and the limits to our appropriation of this mystery.

In both prayers, the reality of what has happened is affirmed. This prayer at the Liturgy of St. Basil, therefore, says, "The mystery of your plan of salvation has been accomplished and consummated to the extent of our power, O Christ our God." The prayer at the Liturgy of St. John Chrysostom is more a prayer of invocation for the completion of God's grace, "You, O Christ our God, ... have fulfilled the whole plan of the Father. Fill our hearts with joy and gladness." The prayer at the Liturgy of St. Basil continues, "We have kept the commemoration of your death, we have seen the figure of your resurrection, we have been filled with your never-ending life, we have savored your inexhaustible delights [i.e. Holy Communion]. Make us worthy of them also in the world to come."

◙ ◙ ◙

We have seen how God acts in the Liturgy, speaking to us, coming to be with us and finally uniting Himself with us through His precious body and life-giving blood. In this way we enter into the life of the Holy Trinity, our sins are wiped out, and we begin a new eternal life. It is fitting and proper that we end the Divine Liturgy by giving thanks to God for "having left nothing undone until you brought us to heaven and gave us your kingdom to come" (Anaphora of St. John Chrysostom). Not only have the bread and wine become the body and blood of Christ, but we too have been changed and transformed through these elements. The words of 1 Corinthians 6:11 may be applied to us after every Liturgy in which we receive Communion to renew our baptism: "Now you have had yourselves washed, you have been sanctified, you have been justified in the name of the Lord Jesus Christ and in the Spirit of our God."

We cannot be faulted, though, for wondering whether this claim is too incredible. It is true and real, but we see it with the eyes of faith and hope and love, which are not sustained by our natural human powers, but only by God acting within us. It is also true that God acts in us in ways that we do not expect or completely understand, as the prophet Isaiah preached, "For the Lord shall rise up ... to carry out his work, his singular work, to perform his deed, his strange deed" (Isaiah 28:21). We perhaps expect God to twist and do violence to His creation to bring it about to His will, but there is a purpose to everything. God works in and through His creation as it is to bring about His wondrous plan. "Through the cross," then, we pray, "joy has come into the whole world," and "by death he trampled upon death." God's work has been carried out in the Liturgy, but in his infinity and eternity, and we are capable of receiving only so much in our here and now human lives and limitations. Perhaps, though, the fullness of God's whole plan will be manifest to us only when we have completed our lives, and have said the final "Amen."

For Your Reflection

1. What do you understand by the phrase, "Holy things for the holy"?

2. What aspect of the mystery of Christ is expressed by the mingling of the consecrated bread and wine before we receive Communion?

3. How are we meant to be transformed by partaking of the Eucharist?

Glossary

Ambon – originally an elevated platform in the center of the church where the Scriptures were read. It is replaced today by a pulpit or by a lectern placed on the solea.

Anamnesis – literally "remembrance;" the remembrance of God's works of salvation expressed in the Anaphora, following the institution narrative and before the epiklesis.

Anaphora – the great prayer of thanksgiving at the heart of the Divine Liturgy; this prayer includes a remembrance of the saving command and acts of Christ, an offering of the holy gifts and an invocation of the Holy Spirit.

Antidoron – blessed bread, distributed at the end of the Liturgy. It is usually taken from the remainder of the prosphoras not consecrated at the Liturgy. Even those who could not share in the Eucharist are welcome to share in antidoron.

Antimension – a cloth imprinted with an icon of the burial of Christ in which a relic is inserted. It rests on the holy table under the Gospel book and is opened before the great entrance.

Antiphon – a psalm sung with a composed refrain.

Bow – an inclination of the head at the shoulders while making the sign of the cross; a *profound bow* includes the extending of the hand to the knees or to the ground.

Canon – a poetical composition of nine odes, each made up of several troparia; it is sung at matins and at other services; the theme of each ode is taken from a corresponding biblical canticle.

Catechumen – a person undergoing official preparation for baptism.

Cherubikon – a hymn sung at the great entrance.

Departed, Liturgies for the – services that include hymns and petitions specifically for the faithful departed; Liturgies for the Departed are not served on Saturday evenings, Sundays, on Great Feasts, and throughout Bright Week.

Divine Liturgy – the title generally given to the Eucharistic Liturgy.

Dogmatikon – a sticheron sung to the Mother of God at the end of the Lamp-Lighting Psalms, composed on the theme of the dogma of the Incarnation.

Enarxis – the beginning of the Divine Liturgy including the great incensation, the litany of peace, and the antiphons.

Entrance Hymn – the final verse of the third antiphon, usually Psalm 94:6 that is sung at the little entrance with the Gospel book; on feasts of our Lord, Psalm 94:6 is replaced by another psalm verse proper to the feast.

Epiklesis – the invocation of the Holy Spirit during the anaphora of the Divine Liturgy asking God to change the elements of bread and wine into the body and blood of Christ and, through them, the faithful who will partake of them.

Eucharist – literally "thanksgiving;" a general term for the Divine Liturgy and for the gifts of Christ's body and blood that are received.

Great Entrance – a procession through the northern door and the holy doors with the gifts of bread and wine about to be consecrated.

Great Incensation – the incensation of the entire church including the holy table, the sanctuary, the icon screen, the icons throughout the church, the faithful, and those serving in the sanctuary.

Hierarchical Liturgy – a Divine Liturgy served by a bishop.

Holy Doors – the central doors of the icon screen on which are depicted icons of the Annunciation and/or the four evangelists.

Holy Table – the table of sacrifice in the center of the sanctuary; on the holy table are the tabernacle, the Gospel book, and the hand cross; beneath the Gospel book is kept the antimension on which the gifts of bread and wine become the body and blood of Christ.

Hymn of the Incarnation – the theological troparion to Christ, beginning "O only-begotten Son," usually sung at the end of the second antiphon; attributed to the Emperor Justinian (527-565).

Icon Screen – the screen adorned with holy icons, joining the sanctuary to the nave; the holy doors are in the center; the northern door and the southern door are also called "deacons' doors."

Irmos – the initial stanza of an ode in a canon relating a biblical hymn to the celebration of the day; on great feasts the irmos of the ninth ode of the matins canon replaces "It is truly proper."

Kontakion – a hymn sung after the troparion or troparia of the Divine Liturgy; this hymn is also sung during the canon at matins and expresses poetically the theme of the day's commemoration.

Lamb – the square central portion of the Eucharistic bread sealed with the letters IC XC NIKA ("Jesus Christ Conquers"); John the Baptist points to Jesus as the Lamb of God (John 1:29,36).

Lamp-Lighting Psalms – the central psalms of Vespers: Psalms 140, 141, 129, 116.

Leave-taking – the final day of the extended celebration of a Great Feast on which the proper hymns of the feast are repeated.

Litany – a series of petitions generally proposed by the deacon with a short congregational response.

Little Entrance – a procession through the northern door and the holy doors with the holy Gospel book.

Little Hours – brief services of praise appointed to be sung at the first hour (6 AM), the third hour (9 AM, preceding the Divine Liturgy), the sixth hour (Noon) and the ninth hour (3 PM).

Liturgikon – a book containing the text of the Divine Liturgies of St Basil the Great, St John Chrysostom and the Liturgy of the Presanctified Gifts.

Magnification – a verse glorifying the feast or saint of the day; in the Divine Liturgy, it usually begins with Mary's words "Extol, O my soul" (cf. Luke 1:46) and precedes the irmos.

Matins – the principal morning liturgical service of the Church.

Mirovanije – literally "anointing with oil;" the practice of anointing the congregation with olive oil and the distribution of bread that were blessed at vespers on certain feasts.

Moleben – a devotional prayer service that includes portions of Matins.

Narthex – literally "small case;" also called the "vestibule," a room of transition from leaving the world to entering the nave; special hymns and petitions at vespers on certain feasts and rituals for catechumens are offered in the narthex.

Nave – literally "ship;" the main body of the temple between the narthex and the sanctuary where the faithful gather to worship.

Panachida – literally "all night;" a brief memorial service for the deceased, derived from the longer wake service of prayer and psalmody that was offered throughout the night in the presence of the bodily remains; it may be sung at a funeral, at the anniversary of a death, or at any other appropriate occasion.

Pascha – literally "*Passover*;" the celebration of the resurrection of our Lord Jesus Christ; this term is also used to designate the forty-day season of celebration which begins on the Sunday of Resurrection and concludes on the day before Ascension Thursday.

Pentecostarion – a liturgical book containing the proper hymns for vespers, matins, and other services throughout Pascha and to the Sunday of All Saints; this term is also used to designate the 50-day period from the Sunday of Resurrection to Pentecost Sunday.

Pre-feast – a day or days of vigil that have hymns of preparation for a Great Feast.

Post-feast – one or more days that have proper hymns extending the celebration of a Great Feast.

Prokeimenon – literally "placed before;" a verse, usually from the psalms, sung as a refrain with one, two, or three verses of the same psalm.

Sanctuary – the "holy of holies;" the area of the church behind the icon screen that includes the holy table and the table of preparation; also called the "*altar*."

Solea – formerly a raised walkway connecting the altar platform to the ambon. Today it is a small extended platform before the holy doors, usually in the form of a half circle.

Sticheron – literally "verse;" a generic term for ecclesiastical hymns sung alternately with psalm verses, particularly at the lamp-lighting psalms of vespers and the psalms of praise at matins.

Table of Preparation – a table at the north side of the sanctuary on which the gifts of bread and wine are prepared for the Eucharistic sacrifice.

Theotokion – a liturgical hymn in honor of the Theotokos.

Theotokos – literally "birth-giver of God;" the main title of the Ever-virgin Mary, Mother of God, defined at the Council of Ephesus in 431.

Triodion – a liturgical book containing the proper hymns for vespers, matins, and other services from the Sunday of the Publican and the Pharisee to Holy and Great Saturday.

Troparion – literally "refrain;" at the Divine Liturgy, a hymn that concludes the third antiphon; this hymn expresses the theme of the day's commemoration; it is also sung at vespers, matins and the hours.

Typical Psalms – Psalms 102 and 145 that, along with the Beatitudes, occasionally replace the three antiphons at the Divine Liturgy. They were originally part of the ***Typica*** service, a monastic rite of receiving Communion in the absence of a priest.

Typikon – literally "order;" a guide to the proper celebration of the liturgical services of the Church; this guide explains what hymns, readings, and rituals are proper in every liturgical service.

Vespers – the principal evening liturgical service of the Church.

Vigil Divine Liturgy – a Divine Liturgy celebrated on the evening before a feast day or Sunday using the proper texts of the feast or Sunday.